CHASING JOY
UNDER A
CATHOLIC MOON

Chasing Joy under a Catholic Moon

A LOVE LETTER TO OUR DAYS

ROBERT BECKER

Marcellus Press

ISBN: 978-1-7351399-1-3 (pbk)

Thanks for the efforts of the following contributors:
Editing services from Patricia Eileen Becker, Esquire
Cover Design by Jack Harrison

Marcellus Press
Robert Becker
Website: chasingjoyunderacatholicmoon.net
Email: robertbecker@chasingjoyunderacatholicmoon.net

*This book is dedicated to all those, who in the pursuit
of life, liberty, and the maximum amount of fun,
accidentally fall backwards into a state
of joy and redemption.*

CONTENTS

Contents

PREFACE

This story is about a time when America was young, when we looked up to presidents, when God was in charge, when TV fathers came home in suits and ties, and everyone was happy after 22 minutes of sitcom and, we loved with our whole hearts except when we were fooling around, and even then we had the best of intentions except for when girls started wearing bikinis, and rock and roll people no longer combed their hair, and cars got too fast for our own good, and grown-ups didn't, or it seemed like they didn't, know anything about sex and love and sex, except that they had children, a lot of children actually and beer and Boones Farm and Bali Hai wine were the bomb, and we knew everything until we didn't, especially how we lived through it, and even then we could swear that we did know all along except when it came to doing something cool like cutting school in June and coming back with a note from your mother with her exact signature on the note, saying you were out cause you were sick and that you still have a fever which would explain the pinkish hue on your face which is not really a sunburn in case anybody was wondering and if there are questions or curious looks the best policy is just to deny! Deny! And Deny! because we have no knowledge of the beach or yesterday's weather because we still are sick and coughing and need to get back to class ASAP since one feels a bit weak. And there's some serious stuff that happens too, but it's not really all that important except that it can bother you and maybe explain why you do the things you do but, in the end, everything wears off eventually. And then you meet the girl and everything sort of changes but remains the same and gets all confusing, and that's the story with a bunch of other stuff happening before, during and after until the story just sort of ends without anybody warning us.

CHASING JOY
UNDER A
CATHOLIC MOON

The First Time I Hit My Father

It was about to happen.

We, my five siblings and I, are assembled around the dinner table. It is a beautiful mahogany, or mahogany veneer table surrounded by eight mahogany looking wooden chairs—not matching, but close enough. My father sits at the head of the table, dressed in tee shirt and plain trousers, looking a bit haggard. I am to his immediate left.

The sun shines in from the two windows, one behind my father, the other behind my younger brother Jimmy who sits next to me. It is the warm season on Long Island and as such there is light through dinner.

My mother enters and exits the dining room from the kitchen bearing server dishes for dinner, religiously scheduled at 6:00 PM, Monday through Saturday. Although my mother is a beautiful, dark haired, woman with an indominable spirit, she is busy now, no time for small talk. Dinner is being served.

I sit, bored, fidgeting with my glass of milk, both elbows on the table, holding the glass to my lips, taking intermittent sips. The sound of slurps that accompany the sips are lost on me, but not so on my father. Like lightning, a concussive force explodes in the vicinity of my chest, my arms, my face. I am blasted into the middle of next week. The glass, the milk, fly through the air. The chair buckles backward and slides off to the side to make room for my thirteen-year-old, ninety-eight-pound frame to land against the wall, only to drop unceremoniously, undignified, to the floor.

Now mind you, as Catholics, we are no strangers to corporal punishment. We are accustomed to the occasional spank or quick clip to the back of the head on the home front, and we are regularly hit at school, for purposes of order and discipline. It is simply part of our culture.

But this blow is beyond the pale.

I pick myself up, right the chair, sit down, stare at my father. It isn't hate, it is beyond any emotion which requires contemplation and forethought. It is rage. Rage is simple. Rage is pure. Rage is beautiful in its singular focus. It only requires a spark—a look, a word, a sneer and it ignites. I had enough of walking on eggshells, navigating his moods, being told that I do everything the hard way or that I always do everything the easy way.

My father's look is one of amusement mixed with disdain. My rage ignites. I do not think about moving the weight from my hind foot to the front foot. I do not think about swinging from the hips. I do not aim for the temple, the nose, or the chin. I simply explode like a piston from a spark. My fist lauds all past injustices by landing knuckles to cheekbone with all the sound and the fury that my corporal self can muster.

Having granted my father license to exact any and every degree of punishment, his hands clasp my throat with an upward thrust, my feet dangle in the air. His eyes are wild, adrenaline courses through his veins, his arms are ripped from pinning me to the wall. My siblings, all except Jimmy, jump up screaming, seeking safety behind their chairs.

And then the moment lays suspended . . . something holds him back.

Although it is my mother who quickly, desperately separates me from my father's grip, when I write the screenplay, the scene will have a translucent, gray, ghost-like figure in a robe with a beard, long hair and sandals who slowly pries my father's fingers from my throat, places his arms at his side, sits him gently back in his seat and escorts me a safe passage to the far side of my father's chair, down the long side of the table, past my sisters and into the living room where I find the stairway and hurriedly escape two flights up to the attic bedroom that I share with my two brothers.

I sit alone on the side of my bed, shoulders slumped, eyes red, suffering through long, deep, involuntary breaths wondering what the hell just happened. I am soon joined by Jimmy, who regales in the retelling of the event. "That was so cool!" he exclaims. "And when you landed that punch, right in face! It was great!"

I am exhausted. I feel no empathy for my father, nor do I find any use for my family in general. I slowly expire as evening turns to night and darkness lays claim to a greater portion of my soul.

It wasn't always like this.

Old Rubber Legs

Returning home from Sunday Mass on a winter day, dressed in my Sunday best, I spy a small patch of ice, a thin layer of frozen water made possible by the uneven break in two slabs of the sidewalk pavement. Only about two square feet in area, this frozen oasis awakens the wild child in my six-year-old self.

With no words, I start the mad dash to bring the ice beneath the souls of my new Buster Brown shoes. In barely a nanosecond, Jimmy follows in hot pursuit. Arms wailing, feet racing, we speed towards this small, freedom-loaded, slippery slope of joy.

Mom and Dad turn their heads. Dad's shoulders stiffen, his chest swells to capture the breath that will carry the counsel to thwart my impending calamity. His arm raises as if to accelerate the words from his lips, only to drop to his side, as a smile comes quickly to his face. He is resigned to my fate.

"There goes old rubber legs", he says to my mother with a subdued but joyful air.

I am upon it. The last step remains. Jumping off, I bring my knees towards my chest, feet together, turning slightly sideways, I attack the ice with my feet, leaning backwards to ensure a smooth, long slide. Sheer joy abounds until the raw pavement abruptly ends my slide and I crash head over heels onto the cement sidewalk. Jimmy follows. A bit scraped but unbloodied, we glance backwards in anticipation of a scolding, only to see their faces shaking back and forth in benign disapproval but with smiles.

The remaining siblings, like chicks in close proximity of their parents, note the acceptance on the faces of their elders and peacefully move on to the next moment.

All is well in Glendale, Queens, a town within a borough within New York City.

Although it's a big city, we live in a small enclave. Saint Matthias' Roman Catholic church and the attendant Catholic grammar school is a short walk from our house.

I am dressed in my navy-blue Holy Communion suit which I received in the spring along with a wristwatch, the usual coming-of-age gift for all first-time communicants in the second grade of Saint Mathias' school. The nuns teach reading, writing and arithmetic but above all, they teach religion and how to make it into heaven.

The heaven part is tricky. You can make it by being good every day but this seems daunting since I can't get through a week without getting yelled at by Mom or Dad. Fortunately, there are a few fast paths to heaven but, unfortunately, they also have troublesome technicalities.

For example, if you wear the scapula that you receive as part of your First Communion, and wear it continuously for the rest of your life, you will proceed directly to heaven. You do not pass GO; you do not collect two hundred dollars; you simply skip the whole line and proceed directly to heaven. A good deal.

A scapula is a small holy picture on a thin strand of linen that you wear around your neck. You are allowed to take it off only for Saturday evening baths.

Jimmy and I are small enough to fit into the single water tub. Dad fills the tub and administers the bath, washes us down to make sure we are clean and not simply splashing around in bathwater. But I never understood the washcloth between the butt cheeks thing, especially when followed by the washcloth across one's back, chest and legs.

Ever the curious wonk, I ask Dad, "Doesn't this just spread the bad stuff all over me?"

"Don't worry, you'll be alright after you dry yourself."

Once the bath water drains from the bathtub, Jimmy and I are left alone to dry ourselves off and get into our pajamas. One night, this costs me my free pass to heaven.

Left to ourselves, Jimmy and I whack each other with our towels. To leave a red mark on your brother's thigh or butt requires skill, cunning, and the right flick of the wrist. Our friendly battle consumes me. We continue our towel duel down the hall and into our bedroom.

The next morning, I awake. I reach for the scapula around my neck only to realize to my horror, that I left it in the bathroom last night. The promise of eternal salvation is null and void. Oh, the agony of a wasted soul crushes my pre-adolescent heart.

But hope springs eternal—there are other fast paths to heaven. According to the nuns, if you say an "Act of Contrition", which is a specific prayer of heartfelt remorse for one's bad deeds, at the moment of your death, your soul proceeds directly to heaven.

When I hear this proposal, I am thinking, "I am in!"

But there is always a "but". In this case, one has to be sincere. It doesn't count if you simply say it. The nuns tell us, "God can see into your soul and He will know if you are telling the truth or not."

Shot down again.

Lastly, one can get a free pass to heaven from attending nine "First Friday Masses." If you go to Mass, a one-hour commitment, on the first Friday of every month, for nine CONSECUTIVE months, you go straight to heaven. What's more, the nuns take each class to the 9:00 AM Mass on every First Friday that you are in school.

Unfortunately, school only covers 10 months of the year. Furthermore, since school starts after Labor Day, you miss the First Friday in September depending upon the calendar, leaving only nine First Fridays in the whole school year. Invariably, a holiday, snow day, or sick day falls on a First Friday, which thwarts the "consecutive" ground rule. The technicalities, coupled with a preteen or adolescent attention span, render this fast path to heaven relatively moot.

However, on one First Friday Mass, a wee posse of seventh grade Catholic boys discovers another technicality that, while it did not offer a free pass to heaven, did allow for a significantly reduced sentence in Purgatory.

Purgatory is like a halfway house for Hell. Since one cannot approach God with sins on or in one's soul, Purgatory is where you burn in the "Lake of Fire" on a temporary basis until the fire cleanses you of all your sins, at which point you proceed to limitless bliss in heaven.

We find the secret for a reduced sentence buried in an obscure prayer book cradled on the back of the pew facing us. My eyes come upon a list of prayers coupled with a corresponding promise of days off in Purgatory. A Hail Mary prayer reduces one's sentence by a week, an Our Father renders a 30-day reprieve, and the Nicene Creed (a very long prayer) reduces one's sentence by 60 days. Furthermore, you can say any prayer multiple times and receive multiple reprieves. For example, seven Hail Mary's reduces one's sentence by 7 weeks.

All well and good but there are two catches: 1) seventh grade boys abhor saying prayers, and 2) one has no idea how long one will be confined to Purgatory and whether all this praying will make a significant dent in one's sentence. Remember, we are dealing with eternity: seven days less than eternity is still a long time.

All appears lost until someone notices the small print at the bottom of the prayer list, "Two days forgiveness for each ejaculation". This revelation turns the whole prayer thing on its head. Suddenly, light breaks through the stained-glass windows surrounding our wretched adolescent pew like a divine light at the end of the redemption tunnel. Salvation beckons since, by seventh grade, we are all practiced at this art.

Suddenly, those 86 questions in the Baltimore Catechism come into focus.

"Who made you?"

"God made me."

"Why did God make you?"

"God made me to share in his infinite love and happiness."

It all starts to make sense at that moment . . . God actually does loves everyone, even fart-joking, sex-snickering, lowlife, seventh grade boys.

It is only later, much later, that we learn that in Christian piety, an ejaculation, sometimes known as ejaculatory prayer or aspiration, is a very short prayer often attached as a form of pious devotion.

My Father's Boyhood,
circa 1936-1944

"It's cold," he thinks to himself as he deposits the last newspaper of his route into the Shubert family mailbox and pushes down hard on his bike pedal for a fast departure. It's a cold afternoon in Glendale, a sleepy little village on the Brooklyn-Queens border set against a bucolic countryside full of farms and cemeteries.

"So what?" young Robert, scolds himself, "it's cold for everyone. I gotta get down to Halsey Street Station to catch the L train before I lose my chance to hawk my last two papers for full price."

He passes the row houses, made up of one long building with residences demarcated by a front door, and on some blocks, a stoop.

"Wet freezing cold is the worst." Snow lands softly but the freezing rain bites the skin exposed by the holes in his gloves. "But four cents is four cents and it will help Mother," he convinces himself.

Following the death of his father the year before, he decides to double up on his paper route to better help Mother to care for him and his younger brother, Richard. He scrounges for stray papers at the office that he can hawk for a few extra pennies—pure profit!

He's in luck, they are just starting to surface from the subway as he arrives. Placing his bike against the subway station columns, he screams, "Get your evening news! Two cents! Hurry! Hurry!"

The sales are mercifully quick tonight. Everyone wants to scurry home out of the rain. He pockets the four pennies and hightails it home, past the farms and cemeteries. The wind blows hard but it's a short ride.

He stuffs the gloves into his jacket pocket before he enters the front door.

"No sense letting Mother see these gloves. She would only want to buy me new gloves and that would only take away from the clothes Richard needs for school this year. Since Father died, I'm the man of the house now, gotta think of Mother and Richard first."

"You have a letter from Brooklyn Tech," Mother says as he enters the front door. "You are accepted. And you are going! No buts about it. I don't want to hear anything about Grover Cleveland High School and your friends."

"It's so far," he says. "It's practically in Manhattan. I'll have to take the subway, round trip. I can ride my bike to Grover Cleveland, or walk, even." He leads with the cost and the convenience but he thinks of after school sports: basketball, football, baseball. And girls. Brooklyn Tech is all boys.

Come September, he walks to Grover Cleveland High School. "Thank you, Jesus!"

. . .

On her knees at her bedside, head bowed, she fingers the beads of her rosary. It's a constant effort to focus on the words of the Hail Mary. It's only been a few months since Robert, her first born, graduated from Grover Cleveland high school. Too often the fear ebbs up from within her and the verses flow and the fingers move unconsciously until they come upon the space for the Our Father. She frets that her prayers will go unheard if she does not concentrate. She focuses attention on the words, "Our Father who art in heaven, hallowed be they name." Her body starts to sway, a little at first, back and forth from the waist up.

"I won't be able to take it" she thinks to herself. Just five years ago, it was Frederick, her husband, taken up into heaven. The thought of losing a child proves unbearable. Her body increases its sway. Her fingers move on to the next Hail Mary. The words come out without thinking, slow, then faster.

Why the Marines? All his friends enlisted in the Army, one in the Navy. She hates the Japanese for what they did. Roosevelt had no choice. he had to do what he did. And now this. The day he graduated from high school he signs up with the Marines. The first ones into battle, the first to die. Today, his eighteenth birthday, he reports to the marine office and he will be gone from her home.

The pain in her hands grabs her attention. Her fingers stopped moving forward. The bead is buried between her index finger and thumb which is red, bruised and bleeding.

"Mother! Mother!" comes the scream from his bedroom. She pushes herself upright, beads falling to the bare floor, and runs.

He sits upright in his bed, his face contorted, fearful, he turns toward her, "I can't move my legs!"

.　.　.

He wishes that she would not make the trip. She must switch several subway lines to get to the Bronx where she boards a bus that takes her across the Hudson River and north through an endless series of small, river-towns. The journey ends at a hospital in Haverstraw.

It's been two years since arriving at the hospital. Much history occurs while he is ensconced in the hospital-world. The allies land in Europe in what the newspapers describe as D-Day. In the Pacific, word of a recent victory at a small island called Midway is good news but the Pacific remains a blood bath. On the home front, rationing overshadows the daily grind and all worry about the return of the depression.

It's better now that he can walk. At first, he was bedridden. Polio left him without the use of his legs. The hospital installs a pull-up bar above his bed. His upper body is the best shape of his young life. Long walks aid and abet the full recovery of his right leg. The disease lays claim to his left leg, no muscle, only bone from knee to foot. He needs a lift in his shoe for a normal gait. He feels lucky: Roosevelt has yet to regain the use of his legs, and others died from polio.

He has mixed feelings about leaving. He will miss the hospital and the fellowship of those not physically perfect. They carried him in the beginning, literally and emotionally. He returns the favor to those who come after him. He takes a small Italian kid under his wing and teaches him basketball and lets him join with the older guys in the weights room. Many of those are waiting for him outside to accompany him on his last bus ride into town where he will meet his mother.

He boards first, with his duffle bag, followed by the fellas. "Stubbs" boards last—a nickname on account of being a double amputee from both elbows. Stubbs offers the bus driver his fare held between his two elbows. The bus driver balks. Big laughs erupt from the fellas. Their camaraderie covers them all like a warm blanket. The bus driver takes the ticket from Stubbs. The bus moves on.

He steps down from the bus into the light of the bus depot. He greets his mother with a firm embrace and a kiss to the cheek. After a quick soda and a sandwich at the local drugstore, they board another bus and head home.

He turns twenty this month. Most of his neighborhood buddies and former girlfriends are already married or engaged. He soon lands his first real job in the city and jumpstarts his adult life. All he needs now is the girl.

The Suburbs

From our first-floor apartment in Queens, we move to a house in the suburbs. We trade our stoop for a patch of green lawn in the front of the house. A driveway for Dad's car displaces the constant search for alternate-side-of-the-street parking. Lastly, the address comes with a backyard quickly furnished with a three-legged BBQ grill and aluminum lawn chairs for grown-ups. Happy days are here.

Life settles into its daily routine—work for Dad, housework for Mom, school and chores for the kids. Towards the end of the work week, Dad frequents a local pub, frequently into the evening.

Home alone, Mom rests on the couch in front of the TV. She welcomes the respite from an afternoon of homework, cooking, bedtime nanny and occasional nurse for her six children. The evening becomes her time.

My two bothers and I sleep in the attic, the third floor. A bed for each of us. Two on one side, and one on the other, each tucked under the slant of the gabled roof. The center of the room, 'No Man's Land,' hosts a large, square, brown rug, good for hiding dirt and blood stains.

A good athlete, Jimmy is a worthy adversary for late night shenanigans. For weapons, we holster old 45 rpm vinyl records, layered with one hit wonders from my older sister's collection.

There exists a single atomic weapon: a 78-rpm record of Alvin and The Chipmunks singing "Jingle Bells." The 78-rpm record is red, which sets it apart from the black 45 rpm singles, but the main difference is the throw-weight of the 78-rpm disk. Where a good toss of a 45-rpm disk simply scratches the faux-wood paneling, the heavier 78 rpm disk makes divots. The thin veneer of faux wood finish is cut away leaving a right, good gash, exposing raw, pale, particle wood. To date, the effect of the 78-rpm disk on the adolescent skull remains untested.

All seems right and proper under God's good night sky this evening.

Jimmy's bed lays directly across the room from mine. Michael, six years my junior, has a bed on the on my side of the room as me. He wisely practices neutrality in this late-night melee.

The first 45 rpm disk flies across the room. It has a casual arc and knocks into the slanted ceiling above Jimmy's bed, falling harmlessly onto his covers.

Comes a pause, our ears on high alert for any sound emanating from the first floor. The TV mumbles on. Jimmy returns fire. The disk flies back to its point of origin.

The war is on.

Winter blankets provide good cover from incoming disks. The intent is to better the adversary, whether it be by a direct hit on the one foolish enough to leave himself exposed, or through attrition—one's retreat into bedtime signaled with no return fire.

The salvos across the room continue in a covert fashion. We aim for each other's bodies as to muffle the sound, out of respect for our mother's peace of mind and the possibility of her vengeance. Inevitably, we hear the voice.

"Stop that racket and go to bed! Don't make me come up there."

Mom tires after daylight. There were no gyms for mothers. No grown-ups ride bicycles. There is only Jack LaLanne, on early morning television—known but never emulated.

With two flights of stairs between Mom and ourselves, we feel safe. The stairs are like our own Maginot line. For Mom to tackle the stairs after a full day with six children is a long shot. We nest beneath our blankets for a short period. A disk traverses No Man's Land like a foul breath of wind between our respective trenches, it begets another skirmish. Disks fly. Paneling scrapes. My brother fights with indomitable spirit.

It is time to end this military action by any means possible. I bring out the atomic. Alvin and the Chipmunks fly across the room. Jimmy engages his ballistic shield, pushing his blanket up in the air in an attempt to deflect the incoming disk from his prepubescent frame. The blanket settles to the bed. The disk passes overhead, unperturbed, taking a divot out of the wood paneling which sends a sonic boom reverberating down the stairways to the first floor.

We freeze. Hold our breath. Wait.

Footsteps. Faint at first. Then louder as she makes it to the second floor. We remain still. There is hope that she stops at the bottom of the stairs to the attic.

The footsteps continue. The sound of shoe leather on the bare wood steps to the third floor creates panic in our hearts: in the rare cases when Mom comes up to the first floor, she's packing at least a curtain rod.

"You know what to do!" I say on a desperate whisper to my brother. "And you gotta scream."

As the eldest brother, I had schooled Jimmy in the appropriate defense. It is our Def-Con 3. One lays on one's back with hands and feet pressed close against the underside of the blanket, appearing asleep but covertly poised for action. When Mom unleashes the curtain rod from on high, one pushes upward on the blanket at the last moment creating a pocket of air between the body and the blanket such that the blanket absorbs the blow from the curtain rod. The trick is to unleash the blanket at the last possible second so that the fury of the moment obscures the defense. And of course, one must scream in agony. To remain stoic can unravel a perfectly good defense.

Mom exacts equal punishment on both of us. Our defense holds, effective and covert.

"If you don't stop it, I will be back with more!" she says in a loud and authoritative voice. "Now go to bed. You have to get your sleep for school tomorrow."

We cower, say nothing.

Mom, weary, descends two flights of stairs. There is no sound of the TV.

After an appropriate silence, I whisper, "See ya tomorrow."

"Yeah," he responds.

In our preadolescent minds, all seems right with the world under God's good night sky.

A Woman of Character
and Substance

Mom does not back down, even back then.

Brushing her hair, Eileen O'Toole readies for school. Dressed in uniform, green plaid skirt, off-white blouse with a clip clasping the blouse close to the nape of her neck.

It looks like rain. She must hurry. It's very important to be on time for fourth-grade at Saint Rose of Lima, Brooklyn, NY.

"I hate the 'look'," she thinks to herself. "Ten seconds late and Sister gives me that look. Like someone's gonna die. Really!"

Entering her classroom as the bell rings, she is quick to take her assigned seat. She sits next to her best friend Maureen McDonnell. Books are stashed below the seat, pencils placed on the desk, she is ready for class.

The day begins.

By afternoon, sitting intermittently upright and slouching back into her chair, she can't hide it. She's bored. Her fourth-grade teacher, Sister Mary Katherine, knows it, Eileen does not care.

This isn't a real movie anyway she insists to herself. There's a high-pitched sound for every scene change. Sister turns a knob on the projector and the next still frame appears. Really! And how many times do we have to see the Passion Play.

They all yearn for Errol Flynn and Olivia De Havilland.

She raises her hand to ask permission to go to the girls' lavatory.

Sister sees her and ignores her.

Defiant, she sits straight up and waves her hand high and straight, adding a wave and a wiggle for effect. Sister sees her and ignores the bratty child again.

"Let this be a lesson in humility for her," Sister ruminates as she turns the knob on the projector.

Eileen lowers her hand in a huff. But the need is real. She has to go. Minutes later, the hand goes up again. It's ignored. Eileen gets up from her desk and marches out the classroom with nary a glance toward Sister. Her classmates are aghast, moving their heads to-and-fro in anticipation of a disciplinary action. Eileen makes a quick exit out the door and down the hall to the girls' lavatory. She arrives too late for a clean visit.

"Oh, I hate her," she says of her teacher upon realization of her sullied state, even though she knows that to hate is to sin. She would love to hit her back if Sister slaps her upon returning to the classroom. She thinks twice. To hit a nun could be a mortal sin. And the knowledge of such a bold act would reach home, and there would be hell to pay.

Walking back to class, the bell rings for dismissal. She dawdles back to her desk ensuring her place at the end of the line for the march out of school. It's imperative that she hide any embarrassment that may be self-evident on the back of her skirt.

She manages a graceful exit and is several blocks away from school before she breathes a sigh of relief. Her hygiene accident remains a well-kept secret.

Suddenly, disaster walks up the street towards her. It is Susan McGillicuddy, a schoolmate. If Susan discovers her sullied state, all the girls will know. Thinking fast, she realizes that Susan was not in school today. She goes on attack.

"You weren't in school today. I'm gonna tell Sister on you!"

"But, I" . . . Susan attempts a response.

Moving forward, closer to Susan who has stopped to explain herself, Eileen raises the decibel level, shaking her finger at Susan, "You weren't in school today! I'm gonna tell sister on you!" Eileen keeps moving forward, incessant with her rant, squeezing between Susan and the storefronts her derriere hidden from view.

Eileen passes Susan with no let up on the rant, shaming Susan with her wagging finger her damp derriere is now safely pointed downstreet and away from Susan's purview. Confused and distressed, Susan quickly puts distance between herself and her mad classmate. Eileen lowers her finger and breathes a sigh of relief and watches until Susan is a safe distance down the block.

Eileen lowers her head. She knows it was mean. She feels for Susan. But it had to be done. The rest of the walk home is uneventful as is class the next day. Eileen uses her milk money to buy Susan a chocolate milk at recess.

.   .   .

She may not always be right but she is a woman who knows what she knows.

It is not as big as Vatican II, but it did register on the Richter scale. A psychiatrist, or a psychologist, or a social worker, or a therapist—some type of lay person comes to the parish rectory to help grown-ups talk through problems. This is seismic.

Prior to this, Catholics had no need for counselors. Catholics had prayer, Sunday Mass, weekday Mass, stations-of-the cross, bingo and confession. And if that doesn't work, there are novenas.

One weekday evening, Eileen and Bob walk up the Saint Aidan's Rectory lawn, passing the statue of the Blessed Virgin poised in prayer surrounded by cherubs. They enter the Rectory office. The meeting is scheduled after hours for purposes of confidentiality—no one must suspect that one has personal problems.

A middle-aged man with an appropriate amount of grey hair ushers them into a room. He sits behind the big desk. Eileen and Bob take the two seats facing the desk.

These sessions do not get anywhere as far as helping Eileen and Bob. As to why . . .

"She doesn't really respect you" says Bob.

"It's true. It's not that I disrespect you," she says holding eye contact with the man. "It's just that I see you as another man who puts his pants on one leg at a time. I am sure that you have a wife who bosses you around at home and scolds you when you deserve it."

"That's true" he replies, looking down and away.

"So why should I take your advice? If you want to know what's wrong, I'll tell you what's wrong. And if you can get him to change, all the good. Until then, this is just talk."

A few sessions later, all agreed to part as friends. So much for counseling.

.   .   .

"Well, Eileen, you should think of Robert" says my father's mother. She admonishes my mother concerning my father's physical and financial well-being. My mother is pregnant with the sixth child. "Did it ever occur to you to pull out?" she asks, her shoulders square and her chin lifted up.

"That's Onanism. It's a mortal sin." Eileen replies with 'the look' without blinking an eye.

"What's that?" Grandma's hand rises to her lips as if she had just cursed God.

"It's in the Old Testament," Eileen adds, locking eyes with her accuser. "Onan pulled out. His seed spilled onto the ground and the Lord struck him dead. Instantly!" she adds, maintaining eye contact.

"Oh Lord," grandma utters, as if it's her last breath.

The following Saturday, at 4:00 PM, the very start of confession, grandma confesses to Onanism, multiple Onanisms, to the shadowy face with a white collar on the other side of the glass darkly.

"And you feel that this is a sin?" he inquires.

"Why yes. The Lord struck Onan dead. Instantly! I don't want to be found outside of the state of grace in the last hour."

There is a long pause. Grandma's hands, clasped in prayer, shake as her fate is held in abeyance.

"Well, we don't really emphasize this anymore," he reassures her. "You can go in peace."

The breath leaves her frail frame like that of a long-distance runner crossing the finish line. Hand to wall, she pushes out and away from the veiled man, breathes back life into her lungs, holds her shoulders square and departs . . . through the nave, beyond the vestibule, down the steps, onto the sidewalk. The sun welcomes her back into the land of the living.

A Hole in One

The sun shines brightly on our blue suburban heaven. Dad pulls the car into the driveway, just short of the garage stuffed with old back-shelf things, to make way, a piece at a time, for baby number six.

I pop open the front passenger door gleefully. I am walking on air, elevated by more than an hour of Coca-Cola and pretzels—my fare at the Colonial Inn, the bar up the block on the corner of the far avenue. Everyone lives between avenues in Mineola.

We're pals, Dad and me. This day we walk up the front steps, through the front door into the living room where all friends and guests are greeted with warm handshakes or quick hugs by the fireplace with birthday greeting cards strewn across the mantel welcoming all comers.

But not today.

Mom walks stridently in from the kitchen, confronting Dad in the center of the living room. "Since when does it take two hours to mail a letter!" she demands loudly.

"For Christ's sake!" he sighs looking down and away. "It's great to be home dear," his voice dripping with sarcasm.

"You're damn right, it's great to be home. And we're not gonna have a home if you keep this up. How many times have I told you? Enough with the bar, enough with the drinking! And do you have to take a ten-year-old into a bar? What are you teaching him?"

I shrink into the background towards the back of the living room by the stairs. It's important to be quiet, to become one with the beige wall, a step away from escape upstairs.

"I pay the bills," he shouts back. "I'm entitled to a little of my own time on weekends."

"But it's not just the weekend! It's weeknights now, more out than at home. I'm raising six kids on my own! I need a husband and the kids need a father."

"I bust my hump five days a week. So what if I top it off before I come home to this hell-hole. Maybe if you were a bit more comforting, I would come home sooner."

"Don't put this on me! And IF, maybe I should say WHEN they fire you, where do we go then? We'll have to be out of this house in a month. You tell me, oh Great Man! Where do we go? My sister's basement, upstate? Your brother's apartment in the city?

"Oh, shut up!" he says, and dismisses her with the wave of his hand.

Her face flushed, tears on her cheek, not from sentiment but from rage. A certain resolve comes from within. Never a church mouse, her conscience is clear, her family at risk. It rises up from the place where church and indignation dwell. Not prone to violence, her left hand still rises to her face and the rage turns the hand to a fist. She bites down on her knuckles in an attempt to hold it inside.

But not today.

She wants to stop.

But not today.

She is indifferent to the pain of clenched teeth on skin and bone. The pain offers no quarter. It only offers the refrain of broken promises to futile requests. She only has eyes for the look. His look holds only disdain. Her right hand rises on its own power subject to its own will.

In the next heartbeat, she strikes him across the face.

I feel myself crying. Confused, I am unsure of my stance, my legs unsteady.

Her arm rises again and falls hard upon his features, repeatedly.

Grown-ups don't fight. My young brain searches frantically for explanation. The uneasiness in my legs rises up into my gut. The room spins like I am on a carousel.

Her last blow draws blood across his cheek.

I am outside my body, floating, eye level to my parents. Their faces turn away into the mirror.

Time slows.

She cries. Not in weakness. It is fury, seething, seeking release.

The mirror holds my father's reflection for a moment. It's partly a boy's face in the mirror—that face that gives his widowed mother pennies from selling newspapers during the Great Depression . . . the face of a teenager who refuses his mother's offer for new clothes, deferring to his younger brother. It is the face of an athlete who takes a younger kid under his wing at the hospital. It is the face of a boy who wants to make things better, to fix things. But now it is a man's face, confused and contorted.

The face looks down and away. He says it under his breath, "Jesus." I barely hear it. It sounds like the Jesus of drowning sailors. But it's not. That Jesus brings a peaceful surrender. This Jesus comes from the lips of those trapped in dark rooms and offers no terms of endearment or respite, only the next cold and indifferent breath. But his mother's Jesus answers, reminding him that he must never ever hit a woman.

He turns from her. Looking up, he catches a glimpse of his bloody face in the mirror. He looks away shaking his head in disbelief but his eyes carry defeat, a hollowing out of the soul.

Breath returns.

When they step away from each other, I look towards my reflection in the mirror. I see no one. Nothing but a flat beige wall.

I find myself at the top of the stairs, running, turning into the narrow hallway. I fall face down on a bed, crying, not knowing why. Dad appears at my bedside. He attempts to console me with assurances that things are all right. But my head, the bed, the room are moving, spinning, full of the sounds, the blood and the fury.

He leaves. I am alone in a new world. It's not as if the world has changed, more like it found the right time, the right place, to tell me something. There are no words, only a feel for a space made new inside me. Maybe the space has always been there but now it's filled with the space between my mother and my father. My crying subsides to a whimper. I am tired but not from running or fighting.

I eventually wake from a merciful slumber, in my clothes, in the dark, damp from perspiration. It's evening. I find my own bed and resign myself to a restless night's sleep in clothes, with only the moonlight through the attic window for company.

Outside, the world waits patiently, like every other night, except tonight the man in the moon rises with a pernicious smile. He knows. I know he knows. I must hide it from everyone else.

What's the Big Deal About Throwing Rocks?

I am outside in the sunshine with nothing to do, just kicking a can down the sidewalk. I notice a buzzing sound like a bee, followed by a snap or a light thud. I hear it a couple more times.

Suddenly, it occurs to me that Billy Lowlife is throwing rocks at me from his side of the street! He doesn't even give me any warning to make it a fair fight. That's typical of the sleezy bastard, engaging in a one-sided fight.

He knows you're not supposed to throw rocks. It was one in a proverbial list of things that can poke your eye out or, worse, break a neighbor's window.

He may be tougher than me. The last time we fought, he pushed me down into a puddle. I got up screaming, ready for a go, but he ran away, laughing his head off. I couldn't catch him. He got the better of me.

A resolve rises in me, a surge of red blood from my gut to my soul. I'll get that bastard this time, I swore to myself. I scramble for a few stones on my side of the street as rocks rain down on me from across the street. He increases the distance between us now that I am wise to his game.

The odds of our ten-year-old arms hitting each other with a rock are low. Neither of us have a good pitching arm or any degree of accuracy but we persevere in our salvos of stones. Fortunately, the rocks never reach the houses behind each of us. There is no collateral damage.

And then it happens. I hear his scream. One of my rocks hits him in the chest. He yelps, followed by a whimper and tears. I'm elated. He's crying. He's mad, as if I violated a rule of his game.

He's the tough kid and he gets hit? It is as if I upset the natural order of things. He is the inflictor of pain. I am a foil for his escapades. This time the good guy wins. Billy runs off to his house, crying. It is a moment for me.

I wax triumphant in the warm glow of a summer afternoon, then turn to walk back to my house. Unbeknownst to me, several fathers on my block have coalesced into a small gathering at the house adjacent to my home, my father among them.

At first, I am pleased that my triumph has witnesses. After all, Billy started it. As I walk closer to the group, I see long faces. A sense of foreboding creeps into my heart. But I did nothing wrong. I fought the good fight. He is the bad guy. I am the one who fought back against the tyranny of the tough kid. I stand for truth, justice and the American way!

As I pass by the group, my confidence erodes. I hear the sound of low voices giving way to grave phrases, like "throwing rocks" . . . "poke somebody's eye out . . . "can't have it." My mood darkens.

My father enters our house after me. "Upstairs," he says with a deep growl. This is not good. But I do as I am told and scurry up the stairs ahead of him.

"Into my bedroom," he says with nothing less than an ominous tone.

He grabs my shoulder, turns me around and pushes me down on my knees.

"Pull down your pants and lean against the bed," he orders as he pulls his belt from his waistband.

He takes the belt to my backside.

I have seen this on TV movies, and I have heard vague stories about other kids in the neighborhood getting this treatment, but this is a first for me, for our household.

Time shifts and I am in a strange space. The belt lands repeatedly. He is changing with each whip of the belt. I can sense my father starting to disappear.

The Girls Don't Wanna
Play No More

Spring arrives on Long Island with long, tender arms. There are no mountains, no forests, no rolling pastures but there are streets, sidewalks and beaches. Summer brings the chance for occasional and often fantastic trips to the beach with Mom and Dad.

In the meantime, there is stickball and baseball. Stickball offers immediate gratification at any time in the day. Six kids, three on each side, played out in the street in front of our houses. It makes for hours of screaming, arguments, and endless fun until one is called home for dinner.

Baseball can likewise be played with only six players but baseball requires a vacant lot, or a field. It has to be self-pitching with hitting restricted to right field and everyone has to have a baseball mitt, or be able to trade off with someone from the opposing team. Furthermore, all the players have to trek many blocks to the local lot. And lastly, the bigger, tougher kids need to be elsewhere.

Stickball calls to us.

Each player spills out of the same front door since all the houses are similar except for paint color and the condition of that little patch of green lawn. Each abode is separated by a driveway that leads to a garage, often chock full of old junk imbued with a latent value known only to adults, protecting it from the weekly trash collection.

With the presence of driveways, the streets are practically clear of parked cars, allowing for a wide space perfect for stickball.

Our games are legend and make for strange bedfellows: Billy, the tough kid across the street; Gary and his brother Billy from all the way around the block; my brother Jimmy and I make five, one player short of the minimum for a decent game.

Enter the girls. Tall and slim, they dress variously in dungarees, or shorts, or those in-between pants that end around mid-shin. Their hair is cut short for the summer or tied up in pigtails drooping against striped tee shirts. Generally taller than the boys, especially if they are a year older like my sister Margaret and her friends, they hit the ball like a ring in the bell, frequently instilling much fear and loathing since they can reach the distant sewer and even, on occasion, dribble it towards the second sewer. The girls come to play.

But this summer is different. The girls show no interest in stickball. The loose hand-me-down dungarees and baggy old gym shorts, perfect for running bases under the summer sun, appear less frequently. Pigtails and striped tee-shirts give way to long hair draped over blouses tucked into slacks. The change in fashion is lost on me and my friends. I only know that the girls' new Sunday-go-to-church clothes mean that it's getting harder to field a decent stickball game.

Our world is changing. I wonder if this has anything to do with the Beatles. Guys like the Beatles too but they are a bigger deal for the girls, especially the slow songs. The girls have baseball cards for the first time in their lives, but the cards are filled with pictures of John, Paul, George and Ringo, instead of Mickey Mantle and Roger Marris. And the radio is full of Beatles songs, which is all good except if it interferes with stickball.

Despite desperate pleas from the boys, heads bowed and arms outstretched in a beggar's plaintive fashion, the girls walk by, indifferent to our plight and disappear into one of their front doors never to be seen again for the remainder of the day. The boys, dejected and forlorn, retreat back to the usual places and spaces on their respective blocks.

We have no clue.

The Beginnings
of Knowledge

Two at a time. I never could walk up the stairs. It is a go. Leaping two steps at a time, I force the pine bannister to support my full weight as I propel myself up the stairs.

Reaching the second-floor landing, I stop, a bit winded. It's a small hallway, past my sisters' bedroom then a left into my parents' bedroom. Theirs is actually, a bedroom and a small alcove with a chair for reading by the front window which overlooks the patch of lawn, the sidewalk, our tree, and the road.

The rush and haste of catapulting myself to the second-floor erases all thought regarding my mission upstairs. I wander for a second.

My father's dresser beckons me. A few coins on the top, a church bulletin (procured but seldom read) rests by a deck of playing cards and a crumpled up, near empty pack of Camel nonfilter cigarettes.

The top drawer is thin and full of knickknacks, very unlike the larger, duller drawers full of socks, sweaters, and underwear. The top drawer is mystery—golf scorecards, cuff links, tie clasps, grown-up stuff, man things.

Holy shit . . . a tie clasp unlike all others, longs to be found. I look again. Is it what I think it is? Holy shit, gotta show this to Ralph—who would believe? For now, I have to reassemble all items as I found them, cover my tracks. He can't know that I know. I am sweating, my hands are clammy and a bit unsteady. Was it covered by the golf score card, maybe by the box of cuff links? Gotta make a call and go.

The sound of the side door to the house opening, is like an alarm bell to me. Someone's home. I slip the tie clasp under the golf scorecard, quietly close the dresser drawer, then head down the stairs as calmly and nonchalantly as possible.

There are voices in the kitchen. I turn at the bottom of the stairs towards the porch and out the front door unnoticed.

Sunlight warms me, my breathing slows. I am free, in the clear. I have time. I bet I can get to Ralph's house and back before dinner.

Ralph's gonna love it. A tie clasp with two breasts on it with hands clasped over the breasts. Incredible!

Why would my Dad have something with women's breasts on it? I gotta think this through.

Maybe Ralph would know. He's Italian.

A Portrait of the Artist
as a Young Dweeb

There is no romance about it. Somewhere between third grade and fifth grade, my best friend Ralph, and I learn the bare essentials about the birds and the bees: Exhibit A is inserted into Exhibit B and that's how babies are made.

As to who told us, it was definitely not Mom or Dad. I suspect it was from someone on Ralph's block, which is a quick walk from my house. Ralph's block is a side street, meaning it is sandwiched between two through streets. My block is a through street between two busy avenues that have traffic lights, four lanes, and lots of moving vehicles. Through streets have more car traffic than side streets, hence more interruptions to stickball games, and games of tag can become dangerous.

As a side street, Ralph's block is a better bet. There are more kids on Ralph's block and more interaction between kids of different ages.

Duke Stirrups may have told us. He is one year older than Ralph and me. Duke is cool, good looking, good at sports and popular in school. He later becomes the leading scorer on his Catholic high school basketball team. Wind Duke up and he shoots. Duke rarely passes the ball. He likes to know things that others do not know. And he likes to let you know that he knows what you don't know.

Or it may have been Larry Chasm. Larry is also one year older than us. Larry wears pointy shoes with a higher heel than normal shoes.

He also wears his hair long. Larry is a tough guy with a sensitive side. Larry's friends from other blocks give off a darker edge and I suspect they talk about these things frequently and in the open.

He may have told us, if we asked.

Regardless, we know now and we continually refine our knowledge like blacksmiths putting blades to a grindstone at a moment's notice on any given day.

On one such day, we are lying on the back lawn of a neighborhood church, pleasantly stuffed from eating cake at their Strawberry Short-cake festival, looking up at a blue summer sky next to our bikes. We ride three-speed English racer bicycles with thin tires, although we are aware that the small twenty-inch frame stingray bikes with high handlebars and banana seats are coming into fashion.

"So how do you think it all started?" I ask.

Ralph volunteers his theory. "It probably got its start at the beginning of time when dinosaurs roamed the earth."

"How's that?"

"Well, the cavemen would see the dinosaurs doing it. And then, after a while seeing all the dinosaurs doing it, he would think, maybe I should do this."

I crunch up my face from doubt.

"Sure," he says "cavemen couldn't talk so they couldn't explain it to each other, but they would see all the dinosaurs. It's like people on a farm today who see all the animals doing it."

"It has to be," he insists, "otherwise we wouldn't be here today. There would be no babies."

He has a point and I couldn't think of any other theory. We part friends and leave the subject for another day.

Ralph's point about cavemen not being able to talk was corroborated the following year with the help of Raquel Welch in the movie *One Million Years B.C.* The candy store on the corner of my block advertises for the local movie theater using a screen shot from the current movie.

For a whole week, every time I pass the corner candy store, I could not help but look at Raquel in a wool bikini with all God's gifts on splendid display. Raquel stirs something in my fifth-grade self that was totally absent in my fourth-grade self. I would love her from afar for the rest of my life.

The dinosaur theory fades as Ralph and I come into the knowledge. At some point in fifth grade, we are in the know but not necessarily in the hunt.

True, I am not allowed to see Raquel's movie. *The Long Island Catholic*, a monthly newspaper delivered via the mail to all Catholic households, rates all movies and gives Raquel's movie the lowest rating: "Morally unfit for All." The other ratings were "Morally unfit for Children," or "Morally Unfit for Adolescents." Not even my parents could see Raquel's movie in good Catholic conscience.

Adieu, my sweet. See you in reruns, forevermore.

. . .

It's the mid-sixties. Headlines scream change: Martin Luther King, Jr. and civil rights; Betty Friedan's *The Feminine Mystique* and women's rights; the Vietnam war, and the right to dissent.

A not-so-slow tide of change washes across America, even influencing Saint Aidan's, my grammar school. They held off as long as they could but, gradually, like the sea takes from the shore, the clergy cave: sex education comes to Catholic school.

But first, by way of preparation, the Bishop comes to town. In fifth grade we undergo the sacrament of Confirmation. The bishop gives us all a soft slap on the face, indicative of the hardships that we will face and the trials that we will endure as Catholics, given the imminent rise in testosterone and estrogen.

In sixth grade, the boys and the girls, previously coed are now divided into two distinct buildings with four lanes of fast vehicular traffic between them. Safely separated, all the boys and girls will be provided with the knowledge—albeit, the basic minimum.

One can almost see Dante scripting a banner over our respective doorways, "Abandon all hope, ye who enter here".

But spring, like adolescence, cannot be denied. With the approach of the summer solstice, winter jackets disappear, and more than flowers are budding as the girls approach teenage years. It becomes time for the talk.

Up to this point, sex education consists of the advice to the girls in line with "do not wear patent leather shoes, it will reflect your underwear."

The girls uniform includes a bow tie with two dangling strips of matching fabric, and a metal clasp on the back of the bow tie for purposes of securing one's top button in order to be doubly sure of not inadvertently revealing any flesh below the chin.

For those girls lucky enough to share confidences with the nuns, they are clued into the secondary use of the tie.

"If a boy approaches you," my elder sister was advised, "pull off your tie and thrust the metal clasp in his face and declare, "Begone Satan!"

So it goes with the Catholic version of *The Joy of Sex*.

In our separate building, the brothers of the Franciscan Order, dedicate a science class to relaying the knowledge to the boys. Since the clergy take a vow of celibacy, one never knows whether their knowledge comes from books or experience.

Case in point:

Dave Curzon is called to the front of the class to demonstrate multiplication for the rest of the class.

As directed, Dave multiplies 3 times 23 on the blackboard. Dave lays out the calculation with a stick of white chalk. The correct answer of 69 brings forth snickers from the peanut gallery. Dave demonstrates that he is "in the know" and responds with a bit of swagger which engenders a bolder round of laughter.

"What is so funny?" grates Brother Marian, irritated by the class reaction to the appearance of 69 on the blackboard.

"Nothing Brother," Dave replies with his most innocent deadpan.

"Tell us of the meaning of what you have on the blackboard!" Brother stammers with increasing irritation.

Dave holds his tongue, shifting uneasily, trying to finesse the moment with silence and a shrug.

"How did this start?" Brother Marian demands in a stern tone, as if inquiring into the origins of the latest curse word from the emerging generation.

Dave looks back and forth between the blackboard and Brother Marian a couple of times with a hapless expression.

"Well?" asks Brother Marian, impatiently.

Dave replies, "Well, I guess it started . . . " He pauses, ". . . with Adam and Eve."

Roars of laughter from the peanut gallery.

"Sit down Mister Curzon!"

The Ballad of
Bob and Eileen

It is Saint Patrick's Day. This year the relatives gather at our house. The party progresses in the usual fashion, with one slight exception.

Jimmy and I, along with our friend Johnny, are in the driveway, shooting hoops at a backboard fixed to the garage. Suddenly, my Aunt Margaret's derriere crashes, rudely, through the rear (no pun intended) kitchen window, just as quickly spraying shards of broken glass onto our basketball court.

My Aunt Margaret's derriere retreats back into the kitchen, no doubt, to address more important matters. Practiced in the art of the rapid, full-adrenaline-alert drill, commonly known as the flight or fight response, my brother and I revert to Def-Con One. We exchange knowing glances, just another day at the monkey house.

It so happened that my father and my Uncle Bill, on my mother's side, agreed, after much drinking, to hammer out a difference of opinion via a fist fight. Being chivalrous gentlemen, they relegate themselves to the basement, away from the unknowing women, children and sober men. The basement is well situated for such an event, the floor having a light film of linoleum over head-breaking concrete.

My Uncle Bill is a big, hardy man, more than six feet tall. At five-foot-nine, my father shows a bit short but he compensates with a degree of madness. Fisticuffs ensue.

Moments later, in what I can only describe as a godsend, my father's brother Richard, my Uncle Dick, descends to the basement to find my father perched on top of Uncle Bill with his hands around his throat, banging his head against the floor.

[Decades later, my Aunt Margaret contends that her brother slipped. "Still counts" I replied].

Uncle Dick pries them apart. The men resurface in the kitchen.

The mood rekindles and another pugilistic event becomes apparent to all in attendance. My Aunt Margaret, a respected matriarch in the family, bravely comes between the two men. That is the moment when her derriere comes out to greet us via the kitchen window.

"What is going on in there?" Johnny exclaims.

Time slows, my blood runs cold, I feel the sting of moisture in the air and my fingers press hard against the basketball. It comes up from within, from that space in my soul. It is all but ready to remind me that I am "less than". Before it speaks, I quickly raise the ball up over my shoulder and throw it. Hard! Johnny lets out a yell from the smack of rubber on bare skin.

"Balls In!" I scream. The blood runs warm again as I escape into our ballgame.

Inside the house, my father pursues his adversary to the horror of all guests. Sanity renders Uncle Bill at a slight disadvantage. His sole intent is to take the bum down a peg and to his thinking, protect his sister, my mother—albeit in a relatively problematic way.

"You want to kill me!" Uncle Bill exclaims, not out of fear for he is a physically capable man, but out of shock when he sees that there is no one home behind my father's eyes.

The fight breaks up due to the presence of other grown-ups. Out of curiosity, I wander into the living room. My mother instructs me to escort Uncle Bill and Aunt Evelyn, to their car. Curbside, Uncle Bill advises me in a slow, slightly inebriated drawl, "Someday you will understand Bobby that . . . "

"Get in the car!" comes a curt and less than loving order from his better half. He obeys. They ride off into the sunset. The remaining relatives escape home.

Night offers a brief respite for my parents.

Early the following morning, Mom holds Dad hostage at the kitchen table. He sits, ragged, shoulders slumped. Two black eyes decorate a sad, sad face. Mom stands firm, bending forward from the waist, right arm raised with her index finger pointing upward from the fist, punching holes in the air to make her points.

"From now on, you are confined to the small bedroom upstairs! You are not to engage, under any circumstances, with the children. And don't come near me. Don't talk to me! Don't touch me! You are a border in this house. That is all!"

He can only look down. The boy who sold newspapers to help support his widowed mother is gone. The young man who overcame polio through strenuous exercise is too tired to fight any more. He exhales the breath of the beaten. This is his moment of truth.

The morning sun rises and through a broken window which coincidently faces east, a ray of light shines onto a clean kitchen floor.

. . .

Tis said that the Lord works in mysterious ways.

I am sure in the thirteen months since the big fight, my father prays for many things. If I had to wager, I would bet that he prays for a million dollars, or some such windfall, to keep the mortgage paid, the credit card bills at bay, a turkey on the table at Thanksgiving and presents under the tree at Christmas. The last thing my father or mother would pray for is a ninth mouth to feed.

Thus, the Lord done did it.

The first six children arrive within an eight-year span. Nine years later, Kate comes into the world, crying.

A fresh wind, we all have a new small someone to love.

Her playpen in our living room is like Grand Central Station. No matter which way one enters the house, Kate becomes the connection and the conductor on the train. Instead of collecting tickets, she hands out free big bags of joy.

Love makes a comeback. Kate is in the house!

Dad saw the light, makes a comeback, and evolves into the likes of Robert Young, of *Father Knows Best*.

. . .

Today, on a table in my family's living room, my father looks out to us from a black and white photograph of himself, bare-chested, twenty years old, at the hospital where he was treated for polio.

On the back of the picture, I write to him:

In this picture, you are the marine you aspired to be
In this picture, you are the marine you never got a chance to be
In this picture, you are a big brother to a younger boy at the hospital
In this picture, you are a high school athlete maturing into manhood
In this picture, you are not yet my father, my mother's groom
In this picture, you are taking lemons and making lemonade
In this picture, you are living the lesson you will pass on to your
  children
In this picture, you are fit, chiseled and handsome
In this picture, you are a god, a child of the Most High*
In this picture, you are your father's son
In this picture, you are your mother's son
In this picture, you are your brother's brother
In this picture, you are my mother's lover
In this picture, you are my father in whom I am well pleased.

. . .

In the meantime, sophomore year in high school arrives with a new cast of characters.

*Psalm 82

Lugnar

Evening approaches. George and I abandon the basketball court and head to his house, the basketball resting atop my hip under my arm. We turn the corner, passing the sump hidden behind weeds and a barbed wire fence, a cesspool that enables the runoff from trim lawns of small capes on small lots into an efficient system of sewers.

A short distance ahead, a tall guy in jeans and a tee shirt with long straight hair over his ears and down to his collar, and with a smirk on his face stands in front of George's house.

"I've set up the Malo fight. It's in motion. Let's make some popcorn," the guy says to George. I meet Lugnar, George's neighbor and friend.

Evening turns to night. George, Lugnar, and I sit on the curb in front of George's house. A cool summer night rests upon our shoulders. The stars shine, the popcorn is buttered and salted. All is right with the world.

What's a Malo fight, I wonder to myself? It sounds ominous, like it has something to do with the tough kids of the neighborhood. I might have to put on my mean face and look intimidating this evening (hoping nothing happens). I hate those situations, such is adolescence.

A car careens from around the corner, cutting a wide swath, risking intercourse with the far curb of the sump. The car completes the arc of its turn and pulls abruptly and coarsely into the driveway across from where we sit.

The car door flies open in a callous and careless manner. The man places a foot onto the pavement and pulls his large frame out of the car with all the glory of a sad circus clown and pummels the lawn with staggered footsteps to the front door.

George, Lugnar, and I continue eating popcorn, handfuls at a time.

"Who is that?" I ask. "He leaves quite an impression."

"Mister Malo" says Lugnar, "Just wait. It gets better." For a brief moment, the scent of the sump passes under our noses, courtesy of a cool evening breeze.

Yelling and screaming emanates from the interior of Mister Malo's house. The cops soon arrive, sirens blaring, guns holstered and a domestic violence case incident is managed to a small event unworthy of an official police report. Police drive away, sirens silent.

"That was entertaining," I said. "How did you know there was going to be a fight tonight?"

"I called it in" replies Lugnar.

"Come again?"

"Yeah. On Friday's, if I see his car at the bar, I call up Misses Malo, and after the third 'Who is this', I just yell, 'Ass face!' into the phone and hang up. It helps to have lousy country music playing in the background."

I walk home under the stars, trying to fathom what I just witnessed. To no avail. It's a quick walk up to the avenue. I turn left, three lights and a right turn and I am home. I retreat to the familiar, which offers comfort for the night.

Brightness falls onto Saturday morning. George calls. Lugnar's parents left for the weekend. I heed the siren call and head over around midday.

The sun shines fat and warm. I turn the corner onto George's short block of a half dozen houses on each side of the street. It is like many streets, except that this block is made up exclusively of capes which gives it a feel of a neighborhood onto itself.

Exiting his front door, George meets me on the sidewalk and we proceed two doors down to Lugnar's house. George gives the obligatory knock on the front door and we walk into the living room where Bozo the Clown is conducting playtime on the TV in living color. No one is watching.

Lugnar is in the kitchen. He wears no pants, no shirt, no socks, no shoes, only a towel wrapped around his waist. He is not fat per se, nor is he thin. He has that milky white skin that knows not a ray of sunshine nor the suffering of an occasional push-up. His hair is long and would normally hang down over his collar, just short of shoulder length but today it's wet and on edge, as if he just put his finger in an electric socket.

George and I enter the kitchen. We all exchange nods.

"What are you doing?" George asks.

"Cooking!" he replies.

"What's on the menu?"

"Spinach!"

"But don't we hate spinach?" George queries, using the royal "we."

"That's right!" is Lugnar's terse response. "My parents are away. I plan to eat all the spinach in the house before they get home so they can't make me eat it when they get back!"

I am puzzled but George gives me a look and a slight nod, encouraging me to go with the flow. George had warned me about "Flogic."

Lugnar's name is Flon. He calls himself Brado, but everyone knows him as Lugnar. Lugnar J. Brado, to be exact. His Christian name is long forgotten, buried beneath layers of personal reinvention.

Lugnar, being Flon, is the source and creator of all Flogic which is based on his personal view of the world, not necessarily touched by reason, natural law, or convention.

Lugnar takes from the oven a sheet of aluminum foil upon which rests a lump of spinach. This culinary piece of art appears limited to simply unwrapping a small rectangular box of frozen spinach and dumping it onto the aluminum foil. As Lugnar transports the entrée from oven to table, green water spills onto the floor. He spreads the green slime around with his bare foot until it is no longer visible to the naked eye. He sits at the kitchen table, the warm spinach in front of him, and adds salt from a salt shaker.

No spoon. No knife. No fork. Using all the fingers of his right hand, he hoists a lump of warm spinach over his gaping mouth and deposits it repeatedly until it's all gone. Somewhere, Emily Post turns over.

"You look like shit," George says.

"Yeah, it's great," Lugnar replies. "They're gone. I came downstairs like this yesterday, right out of the shower. My hair all freaked out, I stand right in front my parents having breakfast at this table and I says to them," waving his fist in the air, punctuating the point like a lawyer to a jury but with an Alfred-E-Newman expression, 'Ain't I the furrrr-fillment of y'ar dreams?'"

"My Dad looks up, and says, 'Judy, look at your son'".

"'Shut up!' she says to my Dad without even looking up from her paper."

Lugnar laughs out loud.

"It was great," Lugnar says, with an impish grin or that look of the marginally insane. One is never quite sure.

Lugnar rises from the table, retrieves a head of lettuce from the refrigerator, and extracts two pieces of bread from the breadbasket on the countertop. He rips a few pieces of lettuce from the head and places them between the two pieces of bread.

He holds the culinary treat up in my direction and declares, "Tusswich!" He sits back down at the table and commences to eat his tusswich.

I turn a dumbfounded gaze to George, beseeching him for an explanation.

"It's a tusswich," George states, lifting his hand in a slight apologetic fashion.

"It's Flanguage," George explains as Lugnar basks in his glory. "Lugnar feels that the English language has evolved over the last few thousand years, and he believes that it's time to push it back a little, to devolve it, if you will. And of course, he is the one to do it."

There is no less confusion in my expression as I wonder whether I am the only one who didn't take the blue pill this morning.

George goes on to explain, "One gets 'tuss' from the word lettuce and 'wich' from the word sandwich and you have a 'tusswich'. Why use two words when one will suffice?" he explains, as if he holds these truths to be self-evident.

"Exactly!" Lugnar declares.

Lugnar continues, "And then there's the etymology of the word privilege. You get 'priv' from private and 'lege' from privilege and you have privilege!" He states this with no less emphasis, looking straight at me.

"That doesn't even make sense," I insist. "You are taking 'lege' from the word . . . "

He cuts me off in mid-sentence. "You state too many things!" He looks away, and returns his attention to his Tusswich.

"It doesn't have to make sense, Bob," George says in a conciliatory tone.

We are momentarily distracted by the loud sound of a distressed car careening down the street and coming to an abrupt stop.

I race to the large living room window and see a Volkswagen Beetle popping itself into reverse and proceeding backwards at high speed into the driveway of the house across the street. The car quickly and deftly parks itself off of the paved driveway, packed tightly behind a tree and in front of several garbage cans on the side of the garage. A man emerges from the car and proceeds directly into the house via the side door, arms swinging with a definite and purposeful degree of precision.

"Mister Cleary's home" George announces to no one in particular.

"Yeah, Mister Cleary's home. How did you like his little parking routine?" Lugnar asks me with a degree of disdain. "It's the same routine every morning and every evening. He's an engineer, everything has to be exact and efficient. He parks that way so that he doesn't block his wife's car from pulling in and out of the garage. And he leaves the steering wheel turned just right, so that when he gets in the car every morning, he just turns the key, steps on the gas and zooms around the tree and out the driveway. Same drill. Different day".

"George, did you notice, his bumper is dented and the car is running a little louder?" Lugnar asks mischievously. "Last week I was coming home after dark, and I just moseyed up his driveway. It had been a hot day and his car window was open. I pushed the steering wheel a bit to the right. Next morning, he gets into the car, turns the key, steps on the gas and BLAM! Right into the tree. Precious!"

We all laugh, a little at first, then hard.

Such is Lugnar.

Domingo

The sun also rises upon a small piece of asphalt with two basketball hoops at each end, one broken and one unbroken. The dew recedes from the grasses around the blacktop that sprout like onlookers at the gates of a coliseum. Wild things, jackals and lions, will gather to this center stage. And this day too, will serve up its' Christians.

Domingo steps out onto his front stoop to begin the daily odyssey, meeting up with his padres loitering on street corners of a Hillside Avenue that leads them to that hallowed patch of asphalt to do battle over a basketball, with all princes of midair.

His Christian name provided at birth, is George. All his close friends call him Domingo. The genesis of this name and almost all nicknames originate and evolve courtesy of Lugnar J. Brado. Said quickly and without regard, the two G's in the name, George, give way to the harsher and more expedient "Ch" sound. George becomes Chorch, which after a while, sounds like "church". Hence George's nickname becomes "Sunday" which is when one goes to church. Sunday quickly morphs in "Sundy because boy names frequently end with the "y" sound, like Bobby, Johnny, Eddie, etc. And that is how he ends up being called Domingo because Sundy, after infinite repetitions for a quick pass, or an alley-oop play, gets shortened to Sunda which sounds like Santa from which comes Santa Domingo, or Domingo for short.

It is in my freshman year of high school that I befriend Domingo.

In my first class of no particular morning, I fill in and submit a survey that seeks to probe the current feelings and views of the freshman class regarding current events: urban riots, the undeclared war, increasing crime and the shrinking middle class—the usual stuff. I give serious consideration about my views regarding the main problems facing the country. After sufficient reflection and repeatedly changing the priority associated with my top concerns, I complete the survey, tender my response to the teacher and proceed to my next class.

We have assigned seats. I have been assigned to the first row, second seat. Each desk is a single unit composed of a seat, a storage space beneath the seat for books and materials, and a metal bar running along the floor connecting the seat to a flat wooden desktop for reading and writing, complete with an indentation at the top to hold a pen. After placing a few books in the desk storage, I quietly slip into my seat.

Domingo enters. In one fluid motion, he throws a pile of books into the storage space of his desk with a loud bang, parks his slender carcass down in the seat behind me and slams a pencil into the small divot at the top of the desk with such a loud bang that it is heard round the world, or at least throughout the classroom. Sitting upright, Domingo exercises a unique idiosyncrasy whereby he tilts his head quickly to the left as each hair on his head stands upright, tilts left, and then with a smooth downward motion followed by an abrupt upward tilt returning his countenance to the mid-point between his shoulders, his hair shifts and swirls around and settles to the right, all lined up as if recently parted and combed.

Domingo has arrived.

Although not yet a friend, I am intrigued by Domingo. I lean back, turning my head to the side and inquire as to his survey response regarding the top issues facing the country.

"Oh . . . stale bread in supermarkets . . . things like that," he replies clearly, as if inconvenienced by having to spend a precious second on something as superfluous as a survey for an alleged group of authority figures, such as teachers.

Like a thunderbolt, it reverberates in my brain, "STALE BREAD IN SUPERMARKETS!"

These are the moments in life, epiphanies, where one sees oneself in a new light. It is like an invisible dove lands on my shoulder and whispers in my ear, "you are my son and you just may be an insufferable dweeb."

My gaze turns back to Domingo. He is not a dweeb. He is irreverent, funny, and unencumbered by the weight of expectations, tradition and homework. This alternative state of being confronts me like a ton of bricks: Domingo is cool.

I don't know if Domingo abhors the thought of homework as some kind of fascist infringement upon his free time, or if he simply does not like the look and feel of books under his arm as he walks to and from the bus stop, or worse, into the school building under the watchful eyes of his peers.

Or, is it something simple? By nature, Domingo is free of those qualities crafted in the womb that produce a worried mind. To him, school is nothing more than a place where he must tell the authorities what they want to hear so that he can get on about the business of enjoying life: making friends, playing sports, finding small amusement in those endowed with less talents than himself. His is the pursuit of life, liberty and fun at all costs. As such, Domingo eschews the unpleasantries of work outside the classroom. He walks to and from school with nary a book in hand except for maybe a paperback copy of "The Agony and Ecstasy," for purposes of his own leisure.

Domingo has unique talents. In football, the long pass has a way of finding his hands among other compatriots. Even when a Hail Mary pass hurtles through the ether, hitting and ricocheting among the limbs of a tree overhanging the end zone, the ball miraculously finds its way into Domingo's hands. In basketball, against all odds, his crazy behind the back shot to the basket finds its way off the backboard and through the net. It is uncanny, and unfair to us mere mortals.

This good fortune happens with such frequency that his shots are referred to as "birdshit" since shots of abject desperation do not warrant the respectful title of "pure bullshit." Ergo, Domingo picks up a secondary nickname, "Birdshit McFlee." Eventually he is officially christened with that nickname by a random bird that lets loose its dropping in midair, the likes of which finds its way to the passenger's seat of Lugnar's convertible only to splat smack dab on Domingo's cheek. Lugnar laughs. The gods have spoken! Birdshit McFlee is here to stay.

Cool, however, does exact its price.

Many years later, on a brisk fall day, Domingo relaxes in the back porch of the family house in the company of his girlfriend, Bliss. A breeze ruffles the curtains and cools the room which contains a rattan couch and two rattan chairs, all with large, comfortable cushions. Game 7 of the World Series is playing out on the TV screen: Baltimore Orioles versus the Pittsburg Pirates. Uncharacteristically, all the fellas are nowhere to be seen, but at least Domingo's parents are elsewhere for the day.

With a cold can of Budweiser in his right hand, soft sofa cushions under his butt and his left arm draping Bliss' shoulders, all is right in Domingo's world.

Each team has won its respective home games. The series is tied three games to three. The last game is in Baltimore, giving the Orioles the home field advantage. It's a pitching duel. After seven innings, the Pirates lead 1-0, but as all baseball fans know, pitchers get tired and anything can happen in the last two innings.

As the game progresses, Bliss tires, not from any physical exertion but from boredom. As the same game progresses, Domingo grows increasingly focused.

In the top of the eighth inning, the Pirates attack and increase their lead to 2-0. As the defending World Series champions, the Orioles answer with a run in the bottom of the eighth. With a single inning remaining, the athletic opera approaches its crescendo. Domingo's heartbeat increases in pace. He fastens his grip tighter around the Budweiser can. Drops of sweat appear on his temples.

Bliss is bored beyond belief.

The ninth inning poses a challenge to her feminine wiles. Sitting with legs crossed, her right-hand slips gently, almost accidentally, from the height of her right thigh to rest upon the fly of Domingo's jeans. Domingo is aware but nonplussed. The Orioles call in Pat Dobson, a 20-game winning pitcher, to make quick work of the Pirate's last batters.

The first Pirate batter steps up to the plate. Bliss unzips Domingo's fly. It's a swing and a miss. Domingo is glued to the TV. Bliss picks up Domingo's bat, her blonde hair obscuring the view to what is fast becoming the center field of Domingo's attention.

Dobson puts the next two batters on base. The Pirates are threatening. Domingo is succumbing.

Dave McNally, another 20-game winner, enters the game for the Orioles and retires the last Pirates' batter, holding the Pirates lead to 2-1.

It is bottom of the ninth, the Orioles have three outs left to secure the win.

Bliss works her art. The first two outs go quickly for the Orioles not so for Domingo, as time slows, the television images blur, his grip on the Budweiser loosens.

It's a fastball coming down the pike. The umpire jumps and jerks a strong right arm into the air, the signal for the game-ending strike!

Bliss scores!

Domingo's head careens backwards, he crushes the can of beer in his right hand. Consciousness abates. His last thoughts . . . a Budweiser . . . a Freudian Favor! . . . and . . . the WORLD SERIES!

Underschmidt

A school bus brings each to his designated stop for a short walk home and a quick deliverance from shirts and ties and into schoolyard garb. Domingo begins the walk that collects us towards that patch of asphalt such is a schoolyard basketball court.

He turns left at the end of his short block, pass the Malos' house onto the Schmidt-a-way, which is a quarter-mile stretch of suburban straight-a-way, made famous by Gerard (pronounced Gee-rard, pronunciation courtesy of Lugnar), who is a small suburban lad turned race car driver courtesy of a pint of Bali-Hai wine and an old, second hand Pontiac Bonneville equipped with a Turbo-Hydra-Matic transmission and a 421 cubic inch V8 engine pushing 425 horsepower.

Entering adolescence as a slightly shy person, Gerard accompanies the band of renown on a high school ski trip with overnight accommodations at a Holiday Inn in the Adirondacks . . . a galaxy far, far away, populated by new girls with no names.

No one skis.

All enjoy the greater sport of partying in the vain pursuit of girls, often settling for the simple pleasure of touching a bare breast or falling asleep, drunk and alone in a strange bed. Against this prurient backdrop, someone observes that Gerard is ne'er to be found.

The search for Gerard takes place against the priorities of drinking, chasing girls, bathroom trips, and haphazardly roaming the halls of the Holiday Inn.

Strolling down one such hall, one hears, coming from behind closed doors, the sound of our little friend. Upon opening the door, we find our Gerard undone by a pint of Bali Hai wine and God knows what else, jumping up and down on the hotel bed with a towel tied around his neck like a cape. He continues, oblivious to his new audience, screaming "Underdog! Underdog!" It's a clarion call to a Saturday morning cartoon character who clearly represents an action hero to our inebriated and enthused colleague.

Henceforth, Lugnar knights him Underschmidt.

. . .

We are awake in the wee hours of the morning in Owen's basement, his parents away at their cottage in upstate New York. The beer drank. The night engaged. Some are finished. Some are not. Not yet old enough to drive, we are confined by what is within walking distance.

"What can we do now?" Ralph asks. "Everything is closed."

"Hope springs eternal," says Domingo.

"Why don't we go up to the avenue and see if we can get chased by the cops," I volunteer.

"How does that work?" inquires Underschmidt.

"We go up to the avenue. If we see a cop, we jump up and down pointing at the cop car like we're up to something and take off running." I make it up as I go along. "The cop will think we did something and he chases us. We cut down the side streets and disappear into alleys or backyards before he catches us."

"I'm game" says Ralph.

"Count me in," says Domingo, and Underschmidt seconds it.

When we reach the avenue, we separate into two groups of two and put the length of a block between us. The avenue consists of two lanes eastbound and two lanes westbound, separated by an island.

Domingo and Ralph are first to notice a cop car heading west as they stand on the eastbound sidewalk. They jump up and down! They point at the cop car! They run! The brake-lights on the cop car turn bright red—the cop has taken the bait. The car does a 180 at the next intersection and accelerates into the eastbound lane. Game on!

Domingo and Ralph run down a side street at top speed. Moments later the cop car takes the same turn on two wheels.

Jealous but entertained, Underschmidt and I do a high-five on account of the successful prank. We linger on the avenue for a few minutes. All is quiet. Drawn to hunt like a moth to a flame, we can't help but take a short walk down the block and follow the trail of the cop car. Two kids, the same age and appearance of the perpetrators walking towards the scene of the crime . . . what can go wrong?

It's a dark, cool, summer night. Visibility is good. The side street is quiet. The cop car is about one hundred yards down the road—no siren, no whirling red light on the roof of the car. All is calm. We are two innocent teenagers heading home or taking a stroll in the wee hours of the morning. Again, what can go wrong?

We spy the officer walking back and forth on the sidewalk, looking for something, his car parked alongside the curb.

As we near his car, the officer barks, "You two, hold it right there."

We freeze.

"Into the car," he says with a stern tone.

"What for? We didn't do anything," I say. Underschmidt nods in agreement.

"If you didn't do anything, what were you running for?" he asks with the same stern tone.

"We're just out for a walk. We're not doing anything," Underschmidt replies.

"At two AM in the morning!" he says with contempt. "Get in the car!"

We both balk. This is not in the plan.

At six feet tall and with sideburns and a heavy beard for a sixteen-year-old, Domingo walks calmly down the driveway from the house next door. Approaching the cop, he inquires, "What seems to be the trouble officer?"

"You live here?" asks the cop.

"Just next door. I heard some noise and saw your car parked outside. Can I help?"

"No" says the cop. "Just some kids up to no good."

The cop turns to us, "Get in the car!"

"What for? We didn't do anything."

"IN THE CAR!' comes the command. Underschmidt and I acquiesce and crawl into the back seat.

"Oh, the injustice!" I am thinking, but I keep mum. The car takes us off in a huff with us in it.

"I'm going to take you down to the station. You're up to no good."

Underschmidt and I are starting to sweat. Great minds think alike: we are freaking at the thought of our parents picking us up at the police station in the middle of the night. This is not a parent-pleaser. The local police headquarters is one of the larger structures in the neighborhood. In my mind's eye, I see my father's face turning redder with each step up the long walkway designed to intimidate those of lesser fortune.

Only a few blocks drive down the avenue, the cop pulls his car into the police station. He stops the car. He turns his head towards us in the back seat. It's a young face for a cop. He asks again, "What were you up to?"

"Nothing," we claim. "Just out for a walk. Sleeping over a friend's house and couldn't get to sleep yet."

"Ok. I'm going to let you go just because I don't want my sergeant to bust my chops about getting a haircut. I will remember your faces and if I see you again, it's going to be trouble for you. Now, get out!"

We walk back to Owen's house—quietly, slowly, unobtrusively. It's a great homecoming. We wail big laughs at Domingo's story. As he tells it, as soon as the cop car turned down the side street, he ran into the closest driveway and jumped into a large thicket of bushes for cover, which to his chagrin turn out to be sticker bushes. As the cop restrained Underschmidt and myself, Domingo got up before the cop can find him in the bushes, inventing his alibi on the fly.

Ralph, the only child of Italian parents, was more afraid of what his mother would do to him compared with anything from the cop. He ran to the end of the driveway at top speed and sailed over a six foot fence, a feat beyond his usual physical acumen, landing in the next yard and almost killing himself. He doubled back to Owen's house alone, keeping to the shadows with an eye out for the cop car.

The laughter subsides; the beer wears off; we sleep the sleep of early years. The fairies come in the wee hours and christen us Lords of the Night.

Roger

From the end of the Schmidt-a-away, a quick right turn and left turn puts Domingo on Prince Street where he picks up Roger, six-feet four inches tall, ravenously skinny, outgoing, affable, possessed of smooth moves on the basketball court, always had a job and knows the value of a penny.

Very few appreciate the penny, the art behind the craftsman who sculpts the image of the sixteenth president of the United States onto a small dab of copper, or the printer who impresses upon that copper the noble words, "Liberty, In God We Trust, United States of America," but the single most impressive characteristic of the penny is the flat edge that encircles this small piece of art and empowers the singular, most fantastic utility of the penny—the roll.

Unless you have been in Catholic school or perhaps an old English boarding school where headmasters paddle boys' butts, one cannot appreciate the bold sound, and symphonic climax of a penny's roll on a classroom floor.

A low tonal buzz emanates from the back of the room. The roll is quick at first, then slows, capturing the ears of a few discerning students. Rolled by a master, the penny approaches the front of the room and like the final pirouette of a dying swan in an opera, the roll turns into a spin, increasing in speed and decibel level. The crowd focuses its attention. All eyes look towards the penny. Its small orchestral spin offers up the sweetest and loudest chord against the vacuous silence of the classroom. The opera ends at the foot of the teacher.

It is no less than a clarion call of rebellion—someone, somewhere in the room believes in the spirit or freedom, justice, and the art of self-expression, challenging the tenets of administrative law and corporal punishment.

Students hold their collective breath as Mister Corona, the teacher, finishes writing his notes on the blackboard. He turns, "OK. You have had your fun. If I so much as hear another peep, or a disparaging word from anyone . . . you will regret that you came to school today!"

He returns to his writing on the blackboard, his back to the class.

A naval orange hurtles through the air towards the front of the class smashing near the head of Mister Corona with such force that the orange hangs momentarily against the blackness of the board for a small eternity before falling unapologetically onto the floor.

A collective gasp fills the classroom as the teacher turns.

Then, Chuck, notorious class clown, walks from the rear of the classroom toward the front. All are aghast. Chuck picks up the orange, turns to the students, who stare back in disbelief."

"Sunkist!" he exclaims. "Who threw a Sunkist?"

A pregnant silence hovers in the air.

Mister Corona looks at Chuck in disbelief, momentarily stunned.

At first slowly, but eventually, raucous student laughter fills the void.

Mister Corona raises his hands to shoulder height and gently, repeatedly presses down with his palms, signaling a call to order and silence. Chuck retreats to his desk. Everyone knows that this is a capital offense. We await retribution. But Mister Corona moves on.

"Mister McHale, pick up the reading at Letter B."

Roger, aka, Mister McHale, extends his index finger like a conductor's baton, indicates an upbeat and starts singing to the tune of the Beatles' song, "Let It Be".

"Letter B . . . Letter B . . . Letter B . . . Letter B . . . .

As Mister Corona lets his head fall to his chest, the entire class waits for the wrath of Khan. The seconds stretch before we perceive a certain jiggle to the head of Mister Corona. He tries to hide a laugh as his head bobbles and his shoulders slouch. He gives into the moment.

All muffle a quiet sigh of relief.

Roger continues, "Speaking words of wisdom, Letter B . . . Letter B . . ."

A crescendo of laughter erupts, and then . . . small solitary voices of fairies, whisper . . . "Don't let it be forgot, that once there was a spot, for one brief shining moment, that was known as Laughalot."

. . .

Domingo and Roger walk a few blocks to the intersection of Herricks and Hillside Avenues, two major roads, where they pick up Owen Kelly, as Irish as the day is long. Average height with a slim athletic build, Owen is an entertaining combination of a quick wit and a quicker temper. I am the last pick up along the avenue until we come to the schoolyard where we meet up with Mando and the Pimp.

Mando

They say Mando came out of the womb with six-pack abs. He is always the best athlete, or one of the best, in any company and in any sport. He also tries harder than just about anybody. He does not express superiority nor is he cocky. However, he will crack a smile or let out a laugh when we revel in the look of despair on the faces of our cross-town basketball rivals as Mando steals the ball for the umpteenth time and scores another easy lay-up.

The most he says of our rival is, "They gotta learn how to go left too, not just right."

It's a warm spring afternoon when we meet at the asphalt. It is a generous schoolyard. Next to the basketball court, there is a long, wide stretch of grass where we play football in the fall. Beyond are two baseball fields saved for summer. But it is the small patch of asphalt that draws this mixed crowd of young men today, like wild things to a watering hole. The groups are friendly in the sense that they need each other for the sake of a competitive game. But they are also on guard for any slight or insult from someone outside of their crew.

A half-court, three on three pickup game sprouts. Young bodies collide, testosterone flows, moves are made, tempers flare, and limits are tested. The winners stay on the court, losers walk. The next trio mounts the court, taking layups and outside shots as warms ups. In a few minutes the next game begins but this game is different because Jackie Rivers has winners.

Jackie is the starting guard on our high school basketball team. He comes equipped with knee brace, superior skills, outsized ego and temper.

He insists we expand to four on four play since his friend and team-mate Tom Smore has just arrived. Tom is Jackie's wingman on the school team. Tom occasionally saves Jackie's ass by being in the right place at the right time for a quick two points.

Jackie insists that we go shirts and skins. "I don't want any fuck ups!" he yells, loud enough to impart dominance. He is here, a lion among jackals. He shoots from the top of the key for first outs. Nothing but net. It's his ball.

Mando covers Jackie. Mando just made varsity this year. Mando is the future, determined to place Jackie in everyone's rear view mirror. Unbeknownst to the rest of us, this game is really one on one, Jackie versus Mando. We are spectators, jackals to the lions, obliged for the pass, pick, or occasional outside shot.

Jackie inbounds the ball and the game begins.

The ball returns to Jackie for an outside shot—swish, nothing but net. It is the opening gambit of a chess game, or the declaration of his presence: "I am here, look upon my talents and tremble." Jackie swaggers back to the top of the key and inbounds the ball to Tom who provides the pick for Jackie's next shot from deep outside. The attempt to impress and intimidate misses the mark and bounces off the rim into my hands. I quickly relay the ball to Mando all alone at the top of the key. He shoots. He hits. Game on.

It's Mando and Jackie at the top of the key. Mando has the ball. Schoolyard rules require one pass before a shot can be taken at the basket. But Jackie covers Mando close, too close. It is an affront, a dare, an insult.

Their eyes meet. There is no love lost here. Mando hates him for the way he always rubs his knee brace whenever he is bested by an opponent and for the pampering that Jackie requests and receives from the Varsity coach. Mando is all business: no show, no quarter asked, and none given. Jackie wants to stare him down. Mando will have none of it, he stares back.

Mando's heart pumps hard red blood laced with venom for his opponent. His knees bent, Mando crouches like one of the big cats. His glutes press tight against the back of his shorts, his quads ripped and taught, ready to pounce. Mando does not look at Jackie's feet to sense the shifting of his weight nor glance at his hips to see a pivot to right or left. His stare is fixed, eye to eye with no retreat. It's showtime, a time for a lesson given or taken.

In one fluid motion, Mando fakes right and moves left gaining a half step on his opponent toward the basket. We give them a wide berth. Mando leaps into the air for a smooth left-handed layup. Jackie counters with chest to chest collision in midair, a blatant foul, knocking Mando off balance. But Mando's left arm stays true to its trajectory and the ball leaves his fingers for a tempered bounce off the backboard and into the net. Mando makes no mention of the foul. Likewise, Jackie says nothing about no inbound pass. It's a one-on-one game.

The ball trades sides back and forth as the opponents exchange outside shots, drives to the baskets, and insults. Jackie's face gets redder and redder. Mando gives no quarter.

Mando attempts the winning basket with another drive from the left. Jackie jumps to block with another chest foul but Mando leaves him suspended in midair as he drives under and beyond the basket for a quick, smooth, back door layup. Jackie lands with a thud and quick turn, squaring off against his opponent.

Mando refuses the bait and returns calmly to the top of the key. He banishes the vanquished with a loud and bombastic "Losers off!" and calls those waiting in the wings with an equally loud, "Next!". It is a clarion call. The tone and the message are not lost on anyone. Jackie and team slowly depart the asphalt.

A warrior, Mando is not one to back down. A fierce competitor on and off the athletic field. He exchanges his share of blows with an opponent when conditions warrant. Mando does not fire in anger. He is a warrior, but a peaceable warrior.

But there is one incident where Mando acquiesces to the powers that be.

In our senior year in high school, the Vietnam war is going full bore. President Nixon receives the baton from Lyndon Johnson and escalates the war in pursuit of "peace with honor." Young men turning eighteen receive notice from the Department of Defense to report to the local Selective Service office for a physical to determine eligibility for the draft. We all were resigned to the draft.

I am not aware of anyone in our neighborhood who went to Canada, or had the wherewithal to secure a position in the National Guard in lieu of a stint in Vietnam.

Mando, the most capable warrior of our crowd—best athlete, good fighter, of high character—is the first one to get called for a physical.

"How was it?" I ask him. It is a lazy Sunday afternoon. We are sitting in the back room of Domingo's parents' house watching a Knicks game. It's a small crowd, Domingo, Roger, Owen, Mando and myself.

"You gotta go down to a government office in Hempstead," he answers.

"What's that like?"

"It's a big place. First there's a small room where you get checked in and do some paperwork. And then you go into a big, cold room where you take off all your clothes with a hundred other guys and wait in line to get checked out by the doctor."

"That's gotta suck," I reply, but I'm thinking that it's somewhat similar to seventh grade when those of us who didn't have a note from a doctor had to report to the nurse's office for a group physical to ensure that our testicles have dropped. About a dozen boys at a time, strip to our underwear. The doctor is old. His two cheeks have sunk below his chin, and likewise, his belly lost the battle with his belt, resting upon his legs. The nurse beckons us towards the doctor, one at a time. The doctor pulls down your underpants, feels your testicles and asks each to cough, turning our heads to the left and then to the right. It's no big deal—all part of coming of age.

The larger crowd at the draft physical is not unsettling since we have done likewise at the locker room at the town pool where boys and men change into and out of their bathing suits in an open room.

"Yeah, the civil service physical is a pain in the ass," says Mando.

"How'd you do?" I ask in what seems like a superfluous inquiry. After all, this is Mando, the schoolyard warrior, the best athlete. It almost goes without saying that he is classified 1A, fit for duty—grade A USA beef!

"I'm 4F," he replies, denoting the classification of those physically unfit for service.

"What?!" The rest unhook from the Knicks game and turn their gaze towards Mando as if we just broke through into another dimension of space and time, a parallel universe that mimics our own.

"How can that be?"

"They disqualified me for hemorrhoids."

"What's a hemorrhoid? Don't you have to be a grandparent to get them?"

"It's a bump on your asshole."

"So, the doctor has to look up everyone's ass as part of the physical?"

"Not exactly."

There are moments in life that are so illuminating that the time, place and words are etched into one's memory forever. However, there are other moments that are so surreal that the words are lost, the hour and setting diffused, and only the message is retained. This is one such moment for me and perhaps for every man, young or old, when he learns of the digital-rectal exam.

"The doctor did WHAT?!" I am blown away by this new, impersonal and intrusive rite of passage.

Mando went on to explain matters but life was not the same after this epiphany. For me, this put the Vietnam war in a whole new perspective. If drafted, I accepted the possibility of being transferred to the other side of the world, to spend a certain amount of time in a foreign, godforsaken jungle, and even shooting someone, given that they aim to kill me. No rational person likes war but it seems preferable to be one of the quick rather than one of the dead.

But this new revelation proves too much. There was just so much I was willing to do for my country. Possessed of such knowledge, I did everything that I could to delay my physical.

I outlasted the bastards.

President Nixon cancelled the draft soon after I turned eighteen years of age in my freshman year of college. Myself and all other young men born in the same year were not called upon to serve. We were fortunate.

I dodged the digital-rectal exam.

Although the politics of that time suggest that all college students were predisposed towards antipathy for President Nixon, I have since found occasions to offer up a brief prayer of thanksgiving for the man.

And I am in debt to Mando for the revelation.

Sunday Morning
EX-TRA-VAR-GAN-ZAR

It's Sunday and sunny. And humid. It's only 11 AM.

In a small local strip mall, Lugnar pulls his 1967 Chevrolet Impala convertible into the first row of the parking lot facing the storefronts. They are all here.

Dressed in their Sunday best, the Moms and Dads, complete with kids in tow, rush to the bakery in pursuit of hot, fresh Kaiser rolls that flake and crumble to the touch. As the counter person deposits rolls into a clean white bag, another white bag holds warm crumb buns, a delicacy much too valuable to mix with the Kaiser rolls and their poppy seeds.

White bags in hand, they rush to the delicatessen if they only need milk for tea or cream for coffee. Otherwise, it's a mad dash to the supermarket for all the necessary complements to a full breakfast because the supermarket lines grow like weeds on Sunday morning.

Children are already hungry from fasting prior to 10 o'clock Mass. Squeaky Buster Brown shoes, white shirts, dress pants, and tight skirts don't help. A long line coupled with the heat and the humidity can kill or at least crumble hopes of a pleasant post-Mass Sunday morning with the family.

Lugnar, Domingo and I, having obtained snacks from the deli, sit facing the storefronts and watch the drama unfold.

A family of four comes into view. The man shifts uncomfortably in a plain navy-blue suit. The center button on his jacket holds fast, like a dying man on a raft. The starched white shirt chafes his neck. He waits at the curb, holding the hand of one small, plump child with his right hand. The wife dresses in a white, go-to-meeting dress under a pale blue cotton jacket whose buttons have long since given up hope of slipping into the button holes. She is sweating. A second toddler holds fast to her left hand. The family waits for a break in the traffic to retreat to their station wagon, a faux-wood paneled car with a roof rack for family vacations.

Elton John pops up on the car radio. "Don't Let the Sun Go Down On Me" provides the score to the melodrama unfolding before us.

"Look at this guy," Lugnar says with disdain. "You just know that he hates his life. The suit alone is killing him. A plain navy-blue suit just like everyone else. It's like he has given up all hopes of ever doing whatever HE wants to do . . . and for the rest of his life!"

Domingo and I laugh out loud.

"By the looks of him, he hasn't played sports or gone out with his buddies in a dog's age. And his wife, no way he likes her any more. And look at that belt buckle of hers, it's her last hope for a figure. It's only a matter of time before it explodes and the metal flies out like shrapnel."

"Medic! Medic!" Lugnar yells in mock panic.

Domingo and I are roaring in between gulps of yogurt and rice pudding. Our sides start to hurt.

"And the kids," he continues. Look at those sour pusses. They look like they hate their lives already. It's as if the kids can see the future and Mom and Dad got to hold their hands just so they don't throw themselves under a car."

Domingo and I gasp for breath between big guffaws. It's all we can do to keep from upchucking our snacks inside of Lugnar's convertible. It's all too funny; the future a bit frightening.

"And the shoes, plain, black, with a round toe. Did he just get out of Creedmoor Psychiatric, or is he afraid of his boss and he's trying to dress so he blends in and doesn't get noticed?"

"Lugnar, I can't take anymore," I say, half kidding. "Let's go."

He puts the car in drive and we leave, making a point to throw our garbage out the window before we exit the parking lot. We don't want to litter another part of town with garbage from this part of town. It's only right.

"Let's watch the Knicks game over at the Pimp's house," suggests Domingo. "His mother just made an apple pie."

As we exit the parking lot, Elton croons his parting advice,

"You're just allowed a fragment of your life to wander free . . . "

In time, we arrive at the Pimp's house. We are on time. It is our time.

The Pimp

The Pimp's Christian name is David, Dave for short. He is not short, about average height. He has bright blond hair with natural platinum streaks in the summer, light blue eyes, sharp features, a disarming smile and a trim athletic build. Even the guys know that Dave is good looking. No one holds it against him. His nickname is the only one that does not come from Lugnar. He owes his nickname to Barbara Best.

Dave was no stranger to the attention of the opposite sex but Barbara lives in that rarefied world of the picture-perfect surfer girl. Tall with long, straight, blonde hair, a body to die for and a face to launch a thousand ships. Barbara is not the stuff for us mere mortals. Barbara is reserved for the likes of the bodice-ripping, Hollywood-bound captain of the high school football team. I have heard other guys share their plans and schemes about getting Barbara's attention or garnering her affections. The best laid plans of these mere mortals always went astray. Barbara chooses. Barbara decides.

One ordinary day, under clear blue sky, a group of us make the trip from the schoolyard to the delicatessen for a cold drink. Coming our way down the sidewalk from the opposite direction appears Dave and Barbara Best, holding hands. It is summer, her shorts reveal long, smooth legs made for wrapping around you, whether standing or lying on a beach somewhere short of heaven. She smiles. We melt. Dave is unfazed. Proceeding with his usual gate, he gives us a slight nod and walks into the pizza parlor.

We exchange glances amongst ourselves. Bewilderment mixed with awe. As mere mortals, our chins refuse to close the space between our lips. We enter the deli. We buy our sodas. Outside, we realize we did not buy our usual drinks. We exchange bottles until we come to a least-worst allocation of drinks between us. We move on.

We hook up later with Dave at the schoolyard. We are curious.

"She likes me," he nonchalantly explains with the shrug of a shoulder. "I don't know why. She calls me at home today. I don't know how she got my number. She wants to go for a walk, so we get pizza. It's nice. I'm supposed to call her tomorrow."

This affair lasts for several weeks. It ends for the simple reason that Dave did not call. "I didn't mean to NOT call her," he says, "I just got distracted. I forget about what." He doesn't mean to hurt anyone's feelings. It simply becomes "over." Dave moves on. The rest of us are dumbstruck. It's like winning the lottery and not bothering to claim it.

There are other examples of paranormal activity in Dave's vicinity. We are at a bar in the Hamptons. The drinking age is eighteen. We all have phony proof. Domingo, Dave and I step outside onto the front steps—three simple wooden steps. Dave sits down on the steps, crosses his legs in yoga style and lights up a cigarette from the ever-present pack of Winstons in the chest pocket of his tee shirt that pulls tight against his chest. A pretty and buxom girl exits the bar. She descends the steps with exceptional care as if she just received communion from the church of the excessively inebriated. She missteps, she swirls, and then descends in a slow, circular manner. Her arms embrace Dave's torso to break her fall. Her face lands squarely in his crotch. She is nonplussed. She tightens her hug. Her arms pull her in closer. She adjusts her head into his crotch as she would address her pillow, or a sexual favor. She rests as if she is in for the night. They become a couple. You can almost hate him.

This afternoon, we settle ourselves in the basement of Dave's parents' house. We all have the munchies. Dave's mother leaves us a homemade apple pie, complete with paper plates and a knife.

Dave picks up the knife and cuts a single piece for himself. In the process of lifting the piece of pie from the tin and drawing it towards his plate, the pie begins to crumble. With the speed of thought, the trajectory of the pie deftly shifts and lands upon my plate as a crumby shadow of its former self.

"Yours broke" he says with a broad smile. Laughter from the peanut gallery.

Not to be outdone, I take the lit cigarette that I had been smoking, place it between my thumb and middle finger and flick it quickly toward his face from only inches away. It's a pre-emptive strike, precluding any defensive action.

The butt is in motion: at least a burn to his face, at best blindness in one eye. The cigarette tumbles towards him, he smiles. I watch as the filter end of the cigarette comes to land between his two lips. It is as if God and the laws of physics conspire towards his good fortune. He takes the last drag on the cigarette, grabs the butt, and crushes it into a nearby ashtray.

.   .   .

Although Barbara slips out of Dave's summer, he does not mourn. A crow appears at his bedroom window one night to castigate him for his malfeasance. He becomes known as "the Pimp" . . . forevermore.

.   .   .

I have a dream.

We were camping which we do each summer once we can drive. Upstate New York begins with rolling hills then turns to a winding river that cuts a deep swath through plush green mountains.

A half hour in the car, we cross the Throgs Neck Bridge and land in upstate New York. In later years, we would know this area as the Bronx, but to our adolescent and mitigated minds, as soon as we were wheels down on the far side of the bridge, we consider ourselves in the country. And everyone knows that it's safe to drink and drive in the country. There's a cacophony of pops from aluminum cans, like the sound of crickets on summer's eve, followed by the downing of that cool concoction that makes long rides short.

Three hours and two cases later, we reach a campsite. We pitch tents. We lay in sleeping bags, four across. I am at one end of the tent, the Pimp at the far end.

The Pimp tells us a bedtime story of beach-body Barbara. The Pimp goes on to describe things to which mere mortals can only imagine.

Dave eventually turns over, facing the wall of the tent. The story rambles off into low guttural sounds of sleep.

Meanwhile, the three sleeping bags to his flank are punching holes in the sky with each dangling participle of the Pimp's ode to adolescent joy. One by one, each sleeping bag expires like a small volcano and falls into deep, dark restfulness.

It is only a dream but one wakes with the dew fresh upon one's youth.

The Girl

We were born before the Wind. Also, younger than the Sun.

—Van Morrison, "Into the Mystic"

She is akin to the sun but not that which hangs in the sky. More like the sun that dances on the water, waving hello then disappearing only to skip the light fantastic across the ocean waves. Her heart resembles the shore in its embrace of the sea.

Her beauty drapes like a fine, yet casual garment. With eyes like pacific blue water set below long golden hair, a smile that brings warmth to all who wake upon the dawn, slender arms that welcome each day with promise, and a tender figure that attracts boys and young men. She is "all that" in terms of fortune and men's eyes. Her legs, slender and sturdy from childhood classes of ballet and jazz, hint of a subtle strength of soul.

She insists on happiness. She thinks that small, simple bicycle accidents are the funniest thing. She can't help but laugh at feet scraping furiously along the ground, the look of imminent danger and the frantic positioning of limbs helpless to thwart the impending crash of clumsiness and laughing stock. She is free except for that she loves with her whole heart.

. . .

It is creeping up on me, drying up my throat, sweating my palms and weakening me in the knees.

There was an initial feeling of joy when I first learned of my good fortune but that quickly fades upon memories of things past, specifically, freshman dances of last year.

It was 1967, the Beatles sent a tsunami to the American shores via their *Sgt. Pepper's* album. The front cover of the album told the story: the original Beatles look down at the gravesite of old rock and roll while the new Beatles, dressed in slick, fresh psychedelic outfits, herald a new wave of cool.

I was way removed from cool, as I tried to figure out what to wear to the town dance in my freshman year of high school. From my closet, I dug out an orange psychedelic tie that my sister had given me for Christmas, then paired it with my orange corduroy pants and a beige shirt. Fortunately, the dance hall is poorly lit. It's in the basement of a girls' Catholic grammar school—the height of chic. I try to chat up a pretty Italian girl. Although she is kind, my fashion sense apparently contributes to her inability to sustain eye contact. Mercifully, attendance is sparse. But orange-pants-guy haunts me to this day.

"It's been over year since that dance" I remind myself. I am a foot taller now. I lost the baby fat in my cheeks and my shoulders have grown wider than my waist. The orange pants and psychedelic tie are long gone, replaced by jeans, and either white tees or flannel shirts untucked. I have dated a couple of girls, even the pretty Italian girl; early teen affairs that one drifts into and out of, with no hard feelings.

But this is different. She is most beautiful. I am afraid.

As I round the corner, I see the library located in a small glass storefront stuck in between the village municipal office and the firehouse. Down the block from the library is the familiar territory of the schoolyard and the basketball court where players begin to gather.

I am conscious of everything, the pace of my walk, to bop or not to bop, the sweat of my palms, the lump in my throat. I tell myself that I have moved on from my freshman year. But I don't believe it.

It was only yesterday I felt normal and carefree and then the best friend shows up.

I am in the schoolyard engaged in a half-court, three-on-three pick-up game on the familiar asphalt. Our young bodies are making fast breaks, hitting from downtown, sweating profusely, not a care in the world. Winners play, losers walk. Life is good.

Pat, the best friend, walks casually along the sidewalk from the direction of the library. Her gait is steady and her steps purposeful. She stops adjacent to the basketball court and her fingers grip the chain link fence that surrounds the schoolyard and separates the sidewalk from the asphalt. As the game ends, Pat calls me over. We know each other enough to say hello and have the occasional brief chat.

I step off the asphalt and jaunt quickly towards the fence, mindful of the start of the next game—the delay of which can be punishable by heckling and mean-facing from the players.

"Hi. What's up?" I ask, as I lean forward against the fence, interlacing my fingers into the chain-link, my white tee shirt soaked in sweat, holding fast against my body.

"Jules likes you," she responds.

"Who . . . me?" I reply in a halting, staccato manner of disbelief.

"Yes, you. We'll be in the library tomorrow, after school." She breaks away and heads back up the sidewalk towards the library with the same casual and purposeful gait.

Bewildered and in shock, like a dog thrown into a cold pool, I return to the asphalt. The game starts and ends in a blur. My head spins from the revelation. On my way home, shock slowly turns to joy as I conjure up the vision of her light blond hair, blue eyes and smile. How did I get so lucky?

We did cross paths last summer, sort of.

It was at the town pool, the hangout place for those in their early teens. The pool has an upper deck overlooking the pool grounds, with two rows of chairs and a pathway in front of each row. The awning offering shade at one end of the deck is reserved for adults. The rest of the deck is populated with those in their early teen years.

One summer day, I am walking across the front row of the upper deck and come across her best friend Pat, an attractive girl with long brown hair, a slim figure, a quick smile and eyes that make you feel like you are the only person in the room.

I stop. We talk. She excuses herself and turns to her best friend Jules, who is sitting about ten feet further down in the second row of chairs.

"Jules" she calls out, catching her attention. Pat casually points her index finger up in the air. "The song," she says. Gerry and the Pacemakers, the British band ushered into America in the wake of the Beatles, are singing "Don't Let the Sun Catch You Crying."

"I don't see myself crying anytime soon," Jules replies with a smile and a laugh.

"What if Alex breaks up with you?" Pat responds.

Jules' laugh causes her head to tilt slightly back, the sunlight highlighting her blue eyes and blond hair.

"That'll do it!" she banters back with an air cheerfulness at the kidding from her friend.

I only hold my gaze for an instant but I had to linger on her for a moment . . . pretty, cheerful, and a kindness and gentility in the brief exchange. I never met her. I only knew of her as Pat's best friend. Even from afar she touches something within, like the golden ring on the carousel that's slightly out of reach.

I turn back to Pat. She was laughing. I smile. We exchange small pleasantries before the end our conversation. I turn way to continue my walk along the deck, in Jules's direction.

The angel on my right shoulder suggests that I turn to her as I pass and offer up a simple greeting. The angel on my left shoulder takes a skeptical view. "Who are you kidding? She doesn't know you! You'll get the blank stare. Go ahead, embarrass yourself!" These two voices raise hell, as I approach the point for a greeting.

I chicken out. I pass by.

I console myself. "She doesn't know you and even if she returns the greeting and you exchange small talk, you're just going to be one of a dozen boys who want to chat her up in hopes of being her boyfriend. It's best that you said nothing." I move on with my face unbloodied but my head a little bowed. The rest of the day and that summer fades into obscurity.

But that was then. This is now. I am walking towards the town library too quickly for my own comfort.

The initial joy at my good fortune is now kicking at the heels of terror.

I plan to talk to her only briefly. A greeting, a few pleasantries, then move on quickly before my voice wavers and she discovers that I am not what I appear to be. I will pretend that I am looking for a book and escape into the library shelves.

My hand grasps the library door handle and I step inside. The entire library consists of one room. The librarian counter is to the right as you enter and a couple of small round tables are to the left. Just past the librarian counter, Pat and Jules sit at a rectangular table with their backs to the wall, each looking down flipping through the pages of their respective magazines. There is a subtle path from the door, past the librarian counter, along the length of their table and into the rows of book shelves.

I hide my last deep breath and walk as nonchalantly as possible along the path. As I approach the table, Jules looks up from the magazine.

I offer up a "Hi" and pause at her table.

"Hi," she responds, looking up. She looks over to Pat and taps on the page of her magazine. It is an advertisement for sun tan lotion. Her finger rests on the picture of a trim, tanned, good looking surfer boy lying on a sandy beach in front of his surfboard.

"He's cute", Pat replies.

Returning her gaze towards me, she asks, "What brings you to the library?"

"Have to get a book for school," I say without a trace of nervousness. My confidence holds.

"For what subject?"

"History," I reply, pleased with my quick ad lib. I extend the fabrication, "Yeah, we're supposed to read *Tale of Two Cities.*"

"There's an old movie based on that book."

"Oh, didn't know. Maybe it'll pop up on *Million Dollar Movie* someday, but . . . ah, . . . can't wait"

There's a slight pause in the conversation.

"Well, gotta look for my book," I say, spending the last bit of my self-assurance. I nod a good-bye and walk towards the bookshelves.

I pass the library cabinet holding the index cards, the Dewey Decimal system being the last thing on my mind. I am maniacally focused on the gait of my walk, hoping to avoid the hurried pace of a scared rabbit. As I enter the realm of the book shelves, I turn left, into the shelter of the last row of books.

I lean against the book shelf, bow my head and exhale the breath of a four-minute mile, my legs are a bit unsteady and my breathing compromised. I breathe in big gulps of air.

What if she walks back here and sees me like this? My heart beats faster. This could be tragic. A tide of panic rises up in my chest. What was I thinking? Why did I put myself in this position? I'm not even in her league. This has to end badly.

The panic does not subside. It increases at the thought of her coming around the end of the bookshelf, seeing me in my panic. All is lost. If not now, any moment now.

A few moments pass. Then a few moments more. Her face does not peer out from behind the row of books.

My breathing steadies. My heartbeat slows. My mind clears. I realize that I cannot huddle in the back of the library forever that I will have to leave the library eventually. But I will have to pass by her table. The terror tries a comeback. I keep it at bay with a few deep breaths.

I must face her and her friend one more time. It requires a bit of bravery. I must man up. I straighten my back, square my shoulders and with one last deep breath, I walk out from behind the last book shelf. I am back on the path heading towards the front door.

I pass their table. I look over. Jules looks up.

"Take it easy." I say in a calm, nonchalant manner without breaking stride.

"You too," she says and breaks into an easy smile.

Within a few short steps, I am out the front door and the sunlight bursts upon my face. My step is lighter, the air is cool and fresh. It is a beautiful day.

Walking on Sunshine

When did walks become so entertaining? As to when schoolyard basketball became secondary, I am unsure as to the exact date. I willingly suffered snickering and catcalls when I first backed out of winners, grabbed my jacket, and hurried off to meet her and her best friend Pat on the other side of the schoolyard fence.

The crew, left one player short, becomes practiced in replacing me. There are no longer any snickers or jibes from the peanut gallery. They watch my back as I trot past the swings and the monkey bars and turn at the opening in the fence then double-back towards Jules and Pat.

Spring never looks so good. Sunshine paints the town in new colors. Light fills new spaces within me.

We walk onto the avenue and pass Hildebrand's ice cream parlor, the place to go after little league games and summer dances at the town pool.

One block east, the three of us turn onto Broad Street. It is a tree-lined street that runs from the avenue and ends at the town pool.

The current walk down Broad Street offers a deeper and more subdued joy but no less exciting. I am a contributor now to the conversation between best friends but mostly I play privileged onlooker to a world of courtesy, good graces, and the art of laughter extracted from the seemingly ordinary. The stories are fleeting. It is the feeling of warmth and affection that beckons me to be a part of this small clique. Perhaps it is the stirring of a humanity within me, the connective tissue between people, beyond one-up-man-ship, and reckless adolescent joy. They fascinate me, especially her.

We turn onto Pat's block. Polite, well-kept houses with a driveway and garage that form one side of a border for the back yard. A picket fence or hedges offer another degree of privacy to the backyard. We pass the occasional homeowner tending to the outside of his house, occasionally visited upon by the call of his spouse from inside the house. It is a storybook world at home in an ecclesiastical peace. All seems right with the world.

Dropping Pat off at her house, Jules and I continue to the corner then we make a right onto Stratford Avenue, and head back to the avenue.

Conversation and light banter ensue.

"I want to have lots of children," she volunteers. Her step has turned into something between a skip and a walk. Her feet lift a little higher than a walk but short of a skip. There is a subtle joy in her gait. Her arms repeatedly stretch out from her side and in front of her into a relaxed clap as if to accentuate the cadence of her walk.

We are walking alone. It is a time for confidences.

"Maybe six, an even half dozen." Her eyes are looking straight ahead and a new type of joy is reflected in the sparkle of light blue. I look up and away towards the road. Although we exchange glances, there is no need for frequent eye contact. We are in our own world on Stratford Avenue.

My pace is relaxed but I am quietly horrified. Children . . . it is a cold forbidding word to me. As the second oldest in my family, the eldest boy, all I know of children are my siblings, an unruly bunch of rug-rats. I've come home innumerable times to find one of them with my Monopoly game strewn all over the living room floor, the box broken from being stepped on and the play-money scattered God knows where. Other days, I find my baseball mitt in the backyard ruined by days of rain. No one owns up to it—for good reason. Children are anathema to me.

I hold my tongue. She is beautiful and possessed of a certain something. I would sooner suffer the outrageous fortune of children than displease her.

"A house filled with children. Wouldn't it be wonderful?" she asks, looking up into my eyes.

"Oh, sure," I lie. "Yeah, it would be great." The joy in her heart touches mine. It is not like the adolescent joy of boyhood of which I am familiar. It is a deeper joy. It bespeaks of a joy that touches the eternal, a joy that connects one to generations gone before and those thereafter. I can only tuck that thought away for another day. I am intrigued.

Our walk continues. We envisage a life married together, courtesy of the Beach Boys:

> *You know it's gonna make it that much better*
> *When we can say goodnight and stay together.*

The mood is light. We are both sixteen. It is a far-off future . . . marriage, children and saying goodnight and staying together, growing old together.

While tripping this light fantastic, I volunteer a throw away comment, "Of course, as the man, I would pass away first."

Her face lights up in a mixture of laughter and trouble-maker. "Oh no. You are not dying first. I'm dying first!"

"What?", I sputter incredulously, surprised by her comeback to my trite comment. "The man usually dies first," I offer up in the spirit of a math geek.

"Oh no buddy! You're not dying first and leaving me all alone!" she laughs. Waving her index finger in my face, "I'm dying first! And that's all that there is to it" she declares with an end-of-story tone.

Reeling from her cheekiness and searching for a good comeback from the feeble corners of my brain, all I can do is break down and laugh.

"Ok, you can die first," I chivalrously grant her.

"You're damn tootin' I'm dying first," she nods firmly. The debate is closed.

Laughter breaks out between us. It is balm for everything gone before.

I reach out to hold her hand. She acquiesces. Like two escapees from a looney bin, we walk on, smiling. No one can know the shape we're in.

We reach the avenue and turn east for the last mile to her house. After dropping her off, I turnabout and walk two miles home. The sun draws pink and reddish hues to itself as it moves closer to the tops of buildings. The air cools. My steps lighten and quicken. Rarely home in time for dinner, I inhale a hamburger and retreat upstairs before my siblings even finish dinner. Dessert is a possibility if the family is in the honeymoon period relative to Dad's biweekly paycheck. I love Hostess cupcakes, Twinkies and Snowballs but there is a new gravitational force that pulls me to the telephone in the second-floor bedroom.

It's been almost thirty minutes. I call. We talk. We laugh.

Sleep. School. And Repeat.

I'll Watch Cary Grant Movies for Her

"Where ya going, there's still beer left?"

"For a walk. Need some air."

It's Charlie Judge, a new friend, as of tonight. His parents are out of the house. He's home alone minding his younger brother with last-minute friends who appreciate an empty house.

"The night's young. Don't worry, he's not going to tell anyone." He is referring to his brother who just came crashing into the kitchen visibly upset. He looks down at the floor, avoiding eye contact with everyone. Barely a teenager, the brother furiously shakes his hands up and down from his wrists. He clearly suffers. The crowd is too much for him.

They are all strangers to him. Strangers in his house. This is unusual for him. He looks away from Jules and myself, his wrists working overtime to shake the strangers out of his mind.

She's closest. She puts her right hand under the palm of his left hand and gently covers his hand with the palm of her other hand. He still looks down and away. Not at first but soon, his left hand slows, the right hand continues shaking—hard. It's uncomfortable to watch.

"Hey, thanks for the party. We gotta go. She's got a curfew and it's at least a half hour walk."

"OK, suit yourself. We'll carry on without you." He smiles and extends his hand for the good-bye handshake. I grab his hand, look him in the eyes, smile. He's a good guy. I like him.

Turning to her, I say "Let's go."

The brother is calm now. She still holds his hand. It's the soft, two-hand hold that you get from a favorite relative when leaving after a Thanksgiving visit. She gently lets go of his hand.

I grab the doorknob to the kitchen door. A twist and a nod to Charlie, we are out of the house. A quick pivot and we are down the short driveway onto the sidewalk and away into the night.

It's a cold, damp April night. Spring is trying to make an entrance but winter stands in the doorway.

On a whim, I suggest that we cut through some backyards as a shortcut. Some preteen gene is in ascendancy within me from a time when Little Leaguers walking home from a game look for some secret-agent adventure by trespassing through private backyards.

I spy a backyard without a fence, grab her hand, and we are off. We scurry up the driveway, an arms-length away from the unknown homeowner's side door entrance. We make it to the garage and along its far edge to another garage and another house that leads to the next block. We are in luck—no fence. It's a quick left then right down the side of the other garage into another driveway and a line of sight to the far sidewalk.

Barking. Loud barking. A goddamn dog gives us up. Fortunately, he's inside the house. We're safe but we have to pick up the pace to make it around the corner before some rankled homeowner comes to investigate or call the cops on us no-good pranksters.

Two blocks later, laughing, breathing hard, we come to rest on a curb sitting, leaning backwards against a US Post Office mailbox. Her legs are drawn up close to her, she catches her breath and places her arms on her knees. My legs are stretched out into the street, my arms fall to my side, my lungs recovering from the great escape.

"What was I thinking, cutting through backyards?" I ask myself. That's such a ten-year-old boy thing that I would do with Ralph years ago. I hope I didn't expose my inner dweeb to her.

We exchange glances and laugh out loud sharing those moments known only to those of dubious sanity. The curb is damp and cold but we are sweaty and warm. The night air is cold and crisp. The stars take their places in the dome and laugh at the two crazies on the curb.

"Did you ever do this with Rosemary?" she asks between gasps of breath, referring to my previous girlfriend.

"No, I never did. For some reason, I never even thought of it."

"She's very pretty. Do you still like her?"

"She's a nice person but no, I don't like her in that way, not anymore. And besides, I would never compare her to you, or compare you to anyone for that matter. You're you, and you're wonderful."

So wonderful, I think to myself, that I wonder what this beautiful creature sees in me. What do I have to offer? I'm good at math and my friends are a fun bunch of guys. I can tell her about binomials and how I can pick out a sine curve from a mile away. But she is beautiful and petite with a figure that makes me want to throw away spring and hop into summer.

But I find it difficult to talk to her family. Her house is big and beautiful and her parents are warm and welcoming yet I can't find the words for small conversation. I bury myself in politeness.

Her older sister who lives at home is beautiful as well. An older brother holds the conversation at dinners with stories from out West where he rides his motorcycle so close to trucks that he can turn off his engine and glide in the truck's backdraft. How cool is that?

What can I say? Should I mention that my father's station wagon has eight cylinders, or that my Mom makes great mac and cheese? I respond with a smile, a friendly nod of the head, and more politeness.

"I am so out of breath," she thinks to herself. He practically had to pull me the whole two blocks. I am trying my hardest to breathe small breaths and avoid big heaves where he's tall, lean and not at all winded. It was great seeing his old girlfriend at Charlie's house. Tall, thin, with olive skin, she looks healthy and tan all year round. She's sweet but I could do without the thick, dark, hair with beaucoup body. He's smart, with a shy side. A little bit awkward at times but I like that he needs help. And when the boy smiles . . .

"We should get you home," I offer up, "and besides, my butt is getting cold and damp."

He pulls me up effortlessly with his outstretched hand. He mentions his butt. That's the first boy to say something like that. It's a bit crude but from him it seems natural, like we are partners in a conspiracy, or it's the beginnings of an intimacy between us.

We hold hands. The evening closes behind us at the avenue. The damp night begins to warm. We walk the remainder of the way to her home without words.

Once inside, she turns on the TV, located in the small den off the kitchen. "Can you stay for a little while?" she asks. The TV fizzes and buzzes until the picture appears. "Oh! One of my favorite movies. It's near the end. Let's watch it together before you have to go."

"Ok."

We sit on a small couch that holds enough space for two and a half people. My arm is around her shoulders, her head leans against me.

I hate this movie. Towards the end of the story, Cary Grant is supposed to meet the love of his life at the Empire State building but she gets struck by a car. And then, when they finally do meet, she won't tell him about the accident. It's a frustrating movie. Eventually she squawks and there's a happy ending.

The credits roll as she looks up with eyes about to tear, and asks, "Did you like it?"

"Loved it."

The Last Summer

Adjacent to the town pool is the Little League baseball field that was once the center of our preteen lives. The infield diamond of dirt and manicured green grass, the pitcher's mound, and the outfield that seemed to stretch out to infinity abuts a forty-foot high, chain link fence that separates the memories of Little League from the town pool, the place for adolescent firsts: first town dance, the horror of one's first dance with a girl, one's first kiss to the tune of Light My Fire by Jim Morrison and the Doors playing over pool loudspeakers.

The remembrances of Little League baseball fade to gray at this time in our lives. The next generation of preteens take the field.

Pool memories from childhood still linger. I recall pure joy when Dad would take us to the pool at the end of his workday. It was dinner time. No one else was in the pool. Margaret, Jimmy, and I, the older siblings, enjoyed sole possession of the pool and its three diving boards. With only a single lifeguard on the evening shift, we ran, we dove, and we splashed with abandon. Dad swam laps at the wide edge of the pool until it was time to go.

The town pool remains relevant to my teenage crew. The pool is the same, the water just as cold in the morning, slowly turning warm under the sun of a summer day. However, the current use of the pool elevates to that of the weekend night, stag skinny-dipping party. The forty-foot fence provides the appropriate testosterone challenge. Fingers and sneakers interlace the chain-link fence. Teenage sinew propels slim, teenage boy bodies to the top of the fence under cover of a black sky and summer stars. Catapulting over the top, the race downward is fast but prone to scrapes and cuts in what becomes almost one long slide to the bottom, arms and legs moving frantically to cushion the fall.

Touching down on a small patch of green grass bordering the fence, it's a short dash of running and ripping clothes from our bodies, all for the joy of being the first to penetrate the surface of a cold, refreshing, illegal body of water. The first head to resurface claims the virtual laurel wreath with a rebel yell.

But all share in the sheer joy of swimming naked, running naked, jumping naked off low and high diving boards, under a disapproving summer moon. Only laughter adorns the ne'er do-wells. Dressing and climbing back over the fence are almost somber affairs made bearable by the promise of tall tales at beach bonfires regarding the night's exploits which grow bolder and grander with each retelling. Adolescence mischief and innocence commingle in warm summer nights.

Ralph

Today is the day, tonight the night.

It is a cold, clear night. Stars filter through the dark canopy with points of light. Looking up, one might sense the beauty afforded by a benevolent first cause or feel the warmth of something close but this night holds itself aloft, cold and indifferent to the happenstance beneath it. The stars are not even there, just the image of something burning millions of years ago. Only the planets are what they appear to be, for they do not twinkle nor husband a single soul. Theirs is a bleak journey shackled to an indifferent sun, committed to repeat the same path until, one by one, their fate eventually bows to forces of fate and gravity and they disappear into the sun in a nuclear blaze with no eyes to witness one's end. Theirs is no kinship with this night's sky.

Tonight's air is crisp and refreshing. One of those nights fit for snow where if the night sky had the kindness to fall, it would have laid a fresh, clean coat of white on the surface of the suburban lawns, with each stoop introducing the houses, one after the other, like sitting pretty policemen in a row, protecting newlyweds with lit fireplaces, or more likely a lit stove cooking popcorn for children of young parents in front of the TV—a town at peace with itself.

Our breath turns the crisp, cold air into a nectar that surrounds us with that which makes boys into a band of brothers. A bond that sees no end to friendships formed in classrooms, on basketball courts, and for this evening, behind the cover of a few trees and bushes by some drainage pipes that flow runoff into our little suburban forest. A small bunch of trees suffice to hide eight young bucks seeking shelter from

the occasional cop car, or the neighbor committed to the death of friv-
olous pleasures beholden to those sixteen years of age. Each one of us
owns a six pack of Budweiser beer, short or tall boys.

Cheerful, carefree, our breath full with the sweet smell of beer—a
Budweiser by any other name still smells as sweet. Just enough drink
to make one especially carefree but not drunk, for we have a long way
to travel and songs to sing as we traverse the matrix of familiar streets.
It's Friday night. It is ours. We will move through, one to two blocks
south, then several blocks across towards the pizza parlor where we
meet girlfriends and for those without girlfriends, a chance to dream
of a midwinter night's surprise.

We finish our drink in this place that we have nicknamed, "the
graveyard" so named because holds the remains of all our other Friday
nights—Budweiser bottles and Budweiser cans mark the places and
faces of past weekends with the occasional litter of budget beer cans
that signify lean times when minimum wage hours did not suffice for
an appropriate brew. Some of the crew plead for a fast departure from
the graveyard, their counsel egged on by cold hands and feet that want
for movement and quicker heartbeats that bring about the warmth that
courses from one's chest and out to the fingers and toes. We take leave
and approach a main road that forms the southern perimeter of the
graveyard.

It's a four-lane road, two lanes south and two lanes north, a double
yellow line down the center protects both lanes from each other. Again,
the air is cold and crisp, the stars in abundance, a night made for snow
where one could trace the waltz of each snowflake navigating its path
from heaven to heaven-on-earth. But there are no snowflakes. The
night is cold, the stars indifferent to our joy.

A quarter mile down the road and around the bend, Luca sits behind
the wheel of an old car with a broken radio, worn seats and a girl on
his right. I have some prior experience with Luca, the product of happenstance. He once saved my hide from a good whipping.

A few years back, Ralph and I were walking down Willis Avenue,
past the church and in front of the chapel which used to be the main
church. The migration of the World War Two generation from the city
to the suburbs forced the construction of the larger church to address

their needs and their baby-boom children. The chapel currently houses a basketball court, the source of hours and hours of teenage basketball where winners can stay on the court forever.

But that day, the chapel was closed. The front of the chapel with its large entrance doors and twelve slight steps to the sidewalk served as the temporary home of the neighborhood tough guys who were taking a break from hanging out across the street at the corner candy store which offered egg creams, cigarettes, and a back alley with shadows. Perched at the top of the chapel's wrought iron railing, the kind that are built to withstand the bomb, sits Luca. Surrounding and subordinate to Luca were a half dozen of ne'er-do-wells, who were more prone to hit you as soon as look at you. They were spread across the steps in a motley fashion.

Ralph and I have been in similar situations many times. An invisibility cloak is best, or when the crew appears in an agitated state, a preemptive crossing of the street is prudent. Preoccupied with our conversation this time, we realize too late that we are walking right in front the lion's den. We both intuitively know enough to sustain our pace and effect a relaxed gate, covering up a creeping sense of panic, brought about by the presence of those who are now our hosts upon the hallowed ground. Eyes straight, we refuse to register any discernible change in expression or perspective. We walk on.

"HEY YOU!" comes an entreat from one of our hosts. Guided by a mutual sense of urban preservation, we continue, our gate unperturbed.

"YOU DEAF OR SOMEFIN!" comes another inquiry from another of the great unwashed. We are not yet at the midpoint of the chapel steps where fleeing becomes an option. The enemy has us flanked in the rear and foreground. At this point we have to retaliate, or at least acknowledge our hosts. We choose the latter—we engage in eye contact! With the empathetic communication of the nearly-dead, we each gamble a look towards one of the clan while our walk remains steady and undeterred, avoiding any hint of bravery or fear, either of which can incent the savage beasts into action.

And then it happens. It becomes personal.

"HEY RALPH!" says an anonymous member on the steps in a menacing tone.

It's show time! Our adrenaline kicks in. It is fight or flight, both of us more in favor of the latter but knowing that the slightest sign of weakness or cowardice will transform us into their objects of amusement in perpetuity.

Before we could react with a "mean face," or the slightly less aggressive turn of the head with a curled upper lip, we hear, "LEAVE 'IM ALONE! HE'S ITALIAN."

It was Luca.

I never knew how Luca came to know Ralph. Ralph may have been at the school playground on some day when I was not by his side, crossing paths with Luca from near or afar. Maybe Luca's younger brother Angelo, our classmate, mentioned Ralph in passing. Or maybe there was a network of Italian mothers. Ralph's mother was born in Italy. She spoke Italian as her first language and English with a heavy accent. Her cooking may have made her renown. We frequently camped out by her side door, wanting in on the sauce that simmered all afternoon.

Regardless, Luca saves us that day. We did not have to resort to a sneer, a response, an exchange of curses, push backs, fisticuffs—nothing. Hallelujah!

But that was then. This is now. Luca is behind a steering wheel and our whole crew leaves the Graveyard.

Within an ether of brotherhood, we take on the night. Chiseled shoulders, lean torsos, taut loins with strong hindquarters that thrust a loose arrangement of vagabond towards the main road, running and leaping like salmon going up-stream.

The night is clear. The road is dry. Luca waits on a green light. A friend of Luca's inhabits the car in the left lane next to Luca's car in the right lane. The road stretching out from Luca's windshield is the exception to the rectangular suburban grid, pock-marked with stop signs or traffic lights. It's a teenage dream of only flat, dry pavement for at least a mile. The road is perfect for racers' intent, except for the curve.

The light turns green. With a strong grip on the steering wheel, both drivers press their accelerators to the floor. Engines roar, rubber burns, the cars speed towards their fate.

Hidden on the other side of the curve, we are crossing the street in mass. Running and jumping, the Lords of the night are spread across the main road in chaotic order. I have reached the far side of the road when I hear the engines. A few friends are near me, not close by but near in the sense that they crossed the road. Others are late to cross, spread across the road. We hear the engines propelling tons of steel and sheet metal our way. When the cars come around the bend of the road it is immediately apparent that we are caught in the headlights of a drag race. The quick ones scurry to the safety of the far curb. Dave and Ralph stop in the middle of the road on the safe side of the double yellow line, having the good sense not to proceed further into the way of the oncoming vehicles.

In the driver's seat, Luca's heart is pumping fast, adrenaline courses through his veins. His eye is sharp, his fingers tactile upon the wheel, his foot pressing the pedal. There is no call for prudence and no time to apply any skill. The message to the car is speed; speed right now and to the maximum available. In his mind, the car is cutting into the night like a sharp blade. His bumper extends beyond that of his friend's car. His car is faster. He is better than his friend. His is certain that his bravery and skill behind the wheel will best his friend. He is not thinking of the laurel wreath that will descend upon his head at the end of the race, nor the sweet feeling of victory that will announce him as the he enters the pub to reminisce about the race, extolling the tale of what he felt at each specific moment, like the rush when he knows that the race belongs to him. He is in the moment, each moment follows the other, into one singular moment that extends into infinity, purchased with the promise of besting his friend.

As we stand and watch, ours is a momentary mix of fear and exhilaration, perhaps even a brief sense of good fortune, to witness something of this magnitude, the site of two cars racing out of a scene from a James Dean movie. All of us are out of harm's way, either on the sidewalk of the far side of the road or, as with Dave and Ralph, safely on the right side of the double yellow line. Dave is a couple of feet short of the yellow lines and Ralph is in a bit safer position than Dave, a few feet further down road and several feet removed from the yellow lines.

Luca is more alive that he has ever been. His car is almost a full car length ahead of his friend's car. It is exhilarating. The moment approaches to exact victory, to declare himself the winner, the debasing of his automotive rival. His rear bumper clears the front bumper of the other car. The moment is upon him. He pulls the steering wheel to the left with both hands in one single motion and cuts off the other car, exerting his dominance. His car careens from the right southbound lane across the left southbound lane of his rival and veers into the northbound lanes. With that single, quick motion, Luca declares victory and a scream emanates from the beginnings of time across all space and time, the cry of every mother with a child in harm's way.

Across the double yellow line into the northbound lane, Luca's car misses Dave by an eyelash. Not so for Ralph. Traversing a few feet further and deeper into the oncoming lane, the car smashes into Ralph four-square. The center of the front bumper meets Ralph at the knees. The grill and hood intersect with Ralph at the hip. The physics fling Ralph into the air like a rag doll. His torso touches the top of the car and then drops onto the trunk and finally, onto the cold pavement. His body slides like a pinwheel to the side of the road, stopped and collected by the curb, bunched up, motionless, dead.

We are frozen in place.

Dave moves first. He bolts towards Ralph, like a pro running back, he makes quick staccato moves to avoid a new northbound car, barely avoiding his own death a second time. He reaches Ralph's body. Turning to face us, he screams with a banshee's wail, "Get over here!" His face is contorted in panic and horror. His scream awakens us from our stunned disbelief.

Partially out of fear of approaching my best friend's lifeless body and because I am closest to a house, I rush to the front door, knocking frantically until the door opens. I scream, "Call the police! Call an ambulance! My friend has been hit by a car." I rush from the house and cross the street to gather with my friends around Ralph, or at least his body. I am capable of knowing that he's dead but I am not there yet. We are all propelled from the material world into another space where time and reason become untethered. We all reel from moment to moment.

At some point, I notice that there are others surrounding us. The occupants of the northbound car that almost hit Dave, return to find us all in a hyper state of shock and mourning. Luca and his friend also return to the scene. They had stopped their cars up the block to let the girls out who were screaming and crying hysterically. All parties offer solace.

"Dave," I say, crying, reaching my hand out to touch his shoulder, "we have to go to church," as if that would offer us respite from this tragedy. My babbling makes no sense but neither does the night. We are torn from the carefree lives that we inhabited just moments ago. It is only shock that supports us by suspending our belief in the present.

Time begins to shift in big blocks. Police arrive. We are whisked away to the precinct to give our account of the accident. Dave and I are the only witnesses who saw the whole accident unfold. The police summon our fathers to collect us. It is midnight. Owen's father, a New York city cop, is the one to tell us that Ralph is dead. It is not until this point that we digest matters, this new reality. No one slept peaceably that night.

Each of us rise the next day. Ralph is gone forever. I do not know forever. I don't do forever.

We meet up later that day on the avenue, blocks from the schoolyard basketball courts. We approach each other tentatively. Each does his best with his Sunday go-to-church melancholy face because we don't know better. Sadness is foreign. We don't do gloom. We do joy. We do cool. We skip school. We shoot straight. We jazz June. We never die soon.

I smile as we meet on the sidewalk. It's habit, all I know in their company. Laughter arrives misplaced but it's the parting gift of shock as the truth slowly creeps into our lives. Winter is coming and the days are short, offering scant light in the hours after school, especially on overcast days. The sun works its economy, sending warmth and pleasantries to other parts of the world.

Weeks later, after the wake and the funeral, I knock at the side door of Ralph's house. Mr. Albanese, Ralph's father, lets me in the house and escorts me to her bedroom. I sit on a small wooden chair with a thin cushion that offers scant comfort, within reaching distance of Ralph's mother, lying in her bed. I am grateful to Mr. Albanese for the chair, the lone means of support in the room. He hurries back to his paper on the kitchen table, grateful for the brief respite afforded by my presence. He recalls the days, just weeks ago, when kids would ring the bell looking for Ralph. He encourages them to visit. The kids don't ring the bell anymore. No one does. Our crew came to visit one time but most of them only go back a year with Ralph. They don't know the family. It's awkward for them. They don't come back. It's only me now at her side in a dark bedroom.

The shades are pulled. There is scant light and it seems to concentrate around me. It hovers over me, touching the top of my head and shoulders. It descends to the top of my thighs, the remainder falling in pieces below the chair. It is not that there is no light in the rest of the room. It is there, but it is dim. It hangs like a shadow on the rest of the room. Like darkness, sorrow moves to each part of the room, to dim anything that offers up light.

Sorrow also remains. It has no direction in and of itself. It stays in the room. It protects us to some extent. It muffles the sound of crying. It dims the light as if to keep the day at arm's length. There is an absence of grief for grief implies movement, like a bloodied fighter pushing up from the canvass for another chance at the foe. Grief swings fists or lashes out with sharp nails that tender a promise of breaking through the veil darkly. This room knows only sorrow.

The room offers a brief light upon her face, the olive skin grown older in the recent days, the eyes dim like a Rembrandt painting. She doesn't wish ill towards anyone.

"But why did it have to be Ralphie?" she pleads.

I understand her plea. Almost all families in the neighborhood have many, almost too many children. She wrestles with why the Lord has taken her only child.

There are no words. I muster fragments of news about my day and the kids that she may know from the block. Conversation comes hard. She responds with the quiet kindness and gentility of a fading soul. I fidget and shuffle my feet. I visit, for this is what best friends do.

In a few months, my visits come to an end. Ralph's mother is taken to the hospital. She refuses the intravenous from the doctors and nurses. She dies of a broken heart. Mr. Albanese is sent to Italy to visit relatives and "to rest." He shows up months later at my house with an attractive woman at his side. My parents, who barely know him, let him into the house and offer hospitality. We all stand in the kitchen. Mister Albanese leans against the counter. He introduces the woman as his new wife who he met and married while in Italy.

"She's forty years old and never been touched . . . never been touched!" he feels compelled to tell us with the speed and intensity of a man who has experienced too much grief in too short a time.

"In Italy, the single women walk across the veranda on the second floor of their houses every afternoon," he explains. "Her brothers introduced us. Everyone there said we were a good match.".

We all exchange pleasantries. It is a brief conversation. It is the last time I see Mr. Albanese.

My soul wants to blame someone for this tragedy. Luca comes to mind. A few months after the accident, my friends and I are in Mr. Albanese's basement with an insurance representative for purposes of providing witness to the accident. We sit around an old kitchen table with a vinyl top and aluminum legs. Luca attends. Like everyone else in the neighborhood, Luca's family does not have a relationship with a lawyer or law firm. No lawyer would volunteer a candid discussion with the other side of a dispute. But Luca has Catholic parents of Italian descent who sympathize with the suffering of the Albanese family. Luca does what he is told. Luca shows up and offers witness.

Two years later, on another cold damp day in April, Luca comes home from Vietnam in a wooden box under an indifferent sky that makes no attempt to offer solace or explain.

Owen

We are in an all-night diner, a small rectangular structure with an entrance in the center. Our night draws to a close. All six of us are feeling no pain. We endeavor to end the night with a hearty breakfast or burger. To each his own, we order the usual. Owen debates the virtues of the cheeseburger versus the cheeseburger special with lettuce, tomato, and fries. Low on funds, he orders the cheeseburger. During this deep contemplation, Peter, one of the smaller, skinnier and wittier members of our crew emits colorful descriptions of a nearby, slightly Neanderthal teenager who is at the other side of the diner with his own posse.

Peter's wit eventually penetrates the deep, thick skull of the brute who consequently meanders over to our booth. It is his intent to extract a toll from Peter for the provision of such entertainment. Reaching over my shoulder, the brute grabs for Peter, who is seated on the far side of the booth. In a flash, I am up in the brute's face, motivated by a quick and forceful push from Owen. Next thing I know, I am behind the counter, bent over, my face close to a hot grill. At the same moment, a plate flies over the counter and smashes into smithereens inches before my eyes.

I right myself to behold Owen facing off with the Neanderthal in the space between the counter and the booths. I join the rest of us, all out of the booth, standing tall, fists clenched, waiting for the next moment. The Neanderthal's posse stand's several steps behind him by the front door, blocking a quick exit. The brute grabs a ketchup bottle from the counter and smashes the bottle against the edge of the table and thrusts the jagged edge towards Owen. In a blink, Owen wraps his jacket around his left arm for defense against the sharp glass and pulls his right fist up and behind his head, cocked and ready to deliver a death blow.

I am left thinking, "Wow, that is so James Bondish!"

Instantly, two short, muscle-bound men with crooked noses and large forearms come out from the kitchen, clothed in the stained gray garb of kitchen help. They step into our space between the counter and the booths.

"You have to leave now!" they demand in no uncertain terms. "The police are on their way."

The Neanderthal lets the ketchup bottle drop and steps aside. First Owen, and then the rest of us pass single file out the front door.

It's dark. Running through the parking lot behind the diner, I hear the sound of a loud motor. As I make it onto the side street, I watch as Peter drives his Mustang down the road like a madman with the rest of us in hot pursuit. The Mustang slows and accelerates in spurts as each of us takes a turn jumping through the passenger side door. I am the last to catch the car. I throw myself into the back seat, spread across the three laps of my compadres.

There is a moment to breathe, followed by a realization that Peter has put a sufficient number of right and left turns between us and the diner so that we are safe from any police pursuit. It starts with a chuckle, then a laugh, and evolves to large belly laughs at the Neanderthal, ourselves, and a perfectly good ending to a hitherto unmemorable evening.

Someone mentions to our surprise and amusement. "We forgot to pay".

There is a hush as we contemplate potential repercussions since we frequent the diner for many late-night breakfasts.

Speaking slowly as if he is coming upon an epiphany, Owen says, "I shoulda got the special."

Low chuckles grow into bursts of laughter.

Peter

He is the only one without a nickname. Lugnar tries calling him Ustinov, after a large, chubby British actor, but it didn't stick. Peter has the slightest build of all the guys, and is a bit effete. Regardless, Peter is smart, good-looking and funny. And funny goes a long way in high school.

Peter and I have been in similar classes through high school but we are separated by geography. Peter lives in Port Washington, separated from my town by a half hour drive, a walking distance that makes closer friendship impossible until senior year when we get our drivers' licenses.

We share the same homeroom which becomes "religion class" in first period which can include current events or lessons in character. Peter and I occupy the last seats in our respective rows of desks. I am in the row next to the windows. Peter is one row over.

Mister Indelicate, a lay person, is our homeroom teacher, and by default, our religion teacher. He is small for an adult male but sufficiently round to compensate for the lack of height. Today's lesson revolves around "commitment" as exemplified by Mister Indelicate's effort to get a soccer program approved at his former school of employment.

"You won't give up, will you?" laments his principal, as told by Mr. Indelicate.

"No," Mr. Indelicate replies. He pauses and canvasses the room with small, beady brown eyes in an attempt to bring drama to his quest. The room is quiet. He strolls up the aisle towards the back of the room. He stops and turns toward the front, leaning against the back wall.

"No, I won't quit," he says, projecting his voice to the front of the room.

"I won't stop," he reiterates with a slight lisp inherent in the word "stop." An exceedingly small half-bubble of spittle from the mouth of Mister Indelicate springs forth, as if accentuating the teacher's defiance. The spittle manages to catch the upper righthand corner of Peter's desk.

Peter freezes. He is aghast.

Having finished his lecture and allowing sufficient time for the dramatic pause, Mr. Indelicate walks slowly to the front of the room. Turning slowly, a dramatic gesture in his own mind, he advises the class to use the last few minutes to prepare for our next class—as if we care.

Under cover of the noise of shuffling books, clicking pens and whispers, Peter declares, "That bastard spit on my desk. What does he expect me to do now . . . study? . . . hose down the desk? . . . What the fuck!"

I laugh as I usually do, at the drama. One can barely, if at all, still see the miniscule drop of moisture in the far corner of his desk.

Peter continues, "And then the fat fuck escapes up to the front of the room without so much as an apology, or at least a tissue."

I continue laughing at this great injustice put upon Peter.

"He probably wants to get up to the front to be near his pet, Hugh McErin".

Peter is winding up into his own stratosphere. Hugh McErin is a chubby little student in the desk next to that of the teachers—a helpless soul behind thick glasses with a couple of chins that rest upon a portly chest and waist.

"Any minute now, Indelicate is going to give into his rapture for the young boy's flesh and devour him in one lustful pounce" Peter adds to his steam of insults.

The laughing pours from me like a mountain stream. If I don't contain myself soon, I risk drawing attention to myself which in turn can lead to Mister Indelicate to impose the fashion-de-jour of corporal punishment.

Several teachers in Catholic school develop their own style of corporal punishment. Some teachers pick you up by the sideburns. Another hides his hands within the sleeves of his clerical robe and as the hand is quicker than the eye, releases a lightning barrage of slaps to the face before the student can apply defense. Still another uses the lanyard, a thick plastic string hanging around the teacher's neck which holds a coach's whistle, or a crucifix, but can be used as an effective whip to the back of a student's thighs. I received five lashes and that was plenty—it hurts! Some teachers have no need for corporal punishment.

A problem with corporal punishment is that it escalates when applied to an adolescent male population. It becomes a game, even a contest. One day you step into a class and everyone's talking about how O'Connor receives 20 lashes of the lanyard. The next week, Romano tops O'Connor with 25 lashes. My last recollection is O'Shaughnessy with 35 lashes before the teacher senses the competition and moves on to another form of punishment.

Later in life, one of my Jewish friends asks me why Catholic school teachers felt the need to resort to corporal punishment. I advise him, "Since we were all either Irish or Italian, it's not like they could reason with us." He understands.

Back to the spittle.

Peter winds down his obscene string of insults. I catch my breath. I am safe, my laughter undetected. The teacher remains deep in thought.

Anyone else but Peter, would have wiped away the spittle with the calloused part of his hand but then there would be no drama, no laughter.

Prequel to Bees Best Be Not at The Beach

It appears as if he has just learned to walk. The two-year-old is a bit shaky on the legs but determined despite carrying a full diaper inside his little Speedo swimsuit. The mother swims laps in the two lanes of the town pool reserved for adults. It is mid-afternoon. Mom is taking a well-deserved mental health break. The little tot is assigned to an aluminum deck chair, one of a several chairs lining this side of the pool. He has a coloring book and crayons, and water wings on his upper arms, just in case. At each length of the pool, Mom looks up from her swimming to check on him. He has it figured out. When Mom pushes off for the next length of the pool, he jumps off the chair, runs to the edge of the pool, splashes the water with his hand and runs back to his seat. He laughs. Mom is none the wiser.

The performance is not lost on Jules as she watches from the upper deck several yards away. She loves the look of the little legs that have not mastered this five-yard dash, and the arms that wail to and from for balance, and the smile on his face from such brazen acts. Jules is all too willing to play back-up lifeguard to this three-penny opera.

"Do you think that he'll get caught?" Tom Baudi asks as he takes a seat next to her. She greets him with a cordial laugh. It is the middle of summer and he frequently catches her alone and offers friendly conversation. He is a junior to her sophomore. With a slim build, dirty blond hair always in place, and light blue eyes set against a pale complexion, his looks and gentle manner rarely offend anyone. They enjoy each other's company.

He purposely tries to look her in the eyes and avoid the casual glance at her full figure, that is tastefully captured in a modest bikini. She in turn, appreciates the innocent banter while waiting for her best friend. A budding friendship has evolved over the recent weeks. He knows her boyfriend and his friends and their preoccupation with sports. Basketball and softball serve as his partners-in-crime while he ponders how to take this friendship to the next level.

Pat, her best friend arrives with much fanfare. "Jules, we gotta go. Phyllis is crying."

Jules knows what this means. A mean word from Phyllis's boyfriend may be the current problem du jour. Phyllis is upset, yet again, and it is the friends-squad to her rescue—to hold her hand, to bring her back to earth, to comfort, console, and make it all better. Jules rises from her chair but feels disappointed at having to leave Tom. She likes his attention and looks forward to their brief contacts in the warm afternoons of summer.

"Sorry, gotta run," she says with a smile. He smiles in return to let her know that he understands. As she walks hurriedly down the line of deck chairs, she looks back. He waves. She waves back and smiles again.

His attention pleases her. She wonders about his intentions.

.   .   .

Saturday's chores are a memory. Sunday morning church fades from the frontal cortex as well. A sunny summer Sunday afternoon is upon us. My parents fill the barbecue grill with charcoal and lighter fluid. The attendant flames signal the advent of a banquet of hamburgers, hot dogs, coleslaw, potato salad and, watermelon.

Sundays are slow. My friends and I celebrate 10'clock Mass at the International House of Pancakes. If one is lucky, one recovers a Mass pamphlet left on the seat from a prior patron. It always helps to return home with a Sunday pamphlet. One doesn't call attention to it, mind you. A casual drop onto the kitchen table will suffice. If it's noticed, all the better. If not, one doesn't lose any points. It can only help.

I am sequestered in the backyard as the resident "big kid" to watch over the children who arrive in tow with my parent's friends. Jules joins me. She is much loved by my parents and all my siblings.

The burgers and hot dogs are offered up with all the accoutrements. The watermelon and the customary seed spitting duels follow. My parents and their friends retreat into the house for conversation. Jules and I are left with a small crowd of children complete with mustard and ketchup stained shirts and shorts.

There is a ball, large enough for all to see from any distance in the yard and small enough for a child to hug and hold within the confines of one's torso, protecting the ball from being stolen by their peers. The girls are the tallest which provides an advantage and the boys are the most aggressive. I hold the ball aloft from all the jumping children until it is knocked from my hand and the games begin. A boy grabs the ball and runs wildly within the confines of a small backyard until those in pursuit wrestle him to the ground like a pack of wild dogs. One of the older girls absconds with the ball and the ceremony repeats itself until I intervene to prevent World War III. I hold the ball aloft and the game ensues anew.

My heart goes out for Betty, one of the smaller children. Betty is a little bit slower and smaller than the other children but she is oblivious to her state. Eventually, I see to it that Betty gets her chance to run with the ball. Holding the ball aloft for the umpteenth time, I quickly bring the ball down and press it firmly against her abdomen. Betty seizes the opportunity and runs like a wild thing, her eyes alight with the ecstasy of her brief victory run. Ultimately, the pack brings her down. She protects the ball like a lioness to a cub. A boy eventually pulls the ball from her but he cannot take the rouge from her cheeks and the smile from her face. Joy abounds.

Jules smiles at me. She sees into my heart, knows my soul. We bask in the fair game, each child to his or her talents with a playing field made level, for all God's children.

Evening falls and a cool breeze rolls over the small people made tired by a warm summer afternoon. The neighbors collect their children a few at a time and the backyard gives way to night.

I walk Jules a couple of miles back to her house and return home. As my head hits the pillow at night, I wonder how I am so fortunate to have a beautiful soulmate with an even more beautiful heart.

As Jules falls asleep, she concludes that Tom Baudi is only a friend.

The Girl, Continued

Winter is giving way to spring.

The Chevy Impala station wagon starts up with a mind of its own. Several birds take flight from the evergreen trees that line her family's property as I pull into her driveway. The rain from the day leaves the evening cold and damp. As usual, she appears out from the back door of the handsome brick house and meets me before I reach the door. Jules plants a brief kiss on my cheek by way of greeting. It warms me.

We have a date. It has been the topic of much discussion over the last several weeks. She sits close to me. Anyone would love her. I am blessed.

I turn my head, trying to look down the driveway for a clean exit without moving her away. We back onto the road and speed away.

Our car parks, alone except for the trees lined up like soldiers along the edge of the parking lot within the park, keeping out any stray ray of light that may sneak through the clouds from the disapproving countenance of the man in the moon.

My eye catches the flight of a small bird joining its mate on a telephone wire. The birds huddle together against a slight drizzle of rain.

The second row of seats in the station wagon fold flat. We huddle in the back. An old blanket long since demoted to the rank of a picnic blanket offers us comfort and warmth. We claim moments without words, spoken in hushed tones.

All those angels on the head of a pin report to our station wagon. Spreading and folding their wings around us, they offer sanctuary from a cold and damp night. Soon we are lifted up. Ours is a tender and fierce flight to the far side of the sun where sunspots leap out from the surface of the sun like dancers glorifying every aspect of the night. Light around us fractures into all the colors, dimming the stars.

Venus is in ascendancy. Mars is nowhere. Mercury wraps us up in solitude and summons Joy to usher us back from the sun and resettle us gently, warmly into our blanket in the back of an old familiar car. Windows made opaque by our breath offer degrees of freedom and refuge from the night. A peaceable weariness coaxes us to stay until the wee hours. But the cold and wisdom give better counsel. We move on to avoid a harsh awakening from the powers that be.

Starting up the car startles the two birds. They abandon a tentative perch on the wire and wing their way in search of a warm wind for passage to a night's nest.

Riding homeward in an intimate silence, I pull the car into her driveway. I walk around the front of the car and open her door. We walk to the back entrance. There are no lights. There are no words. I hold her firmly and plant a brief kiss on her lips and release her to the night. She pulls me by the lapels of my jacket, back into her. She looks into my eyes and kisses me hard. She disappears into a dark hallway.

I ride home to sleep without dreams.

.   .   .

I open the passenger side door to the Police car, slide onto the seat with my eyes looking down. I steal a sideways glance at him. He has wide shoulders and his police uniform fits tight against a large, trim chest. Just my luck, I have to cross paths with the "Hulk" of the East Hills Police Department.

It's dark. I can't see anything through the car windows. My car is a few feet behind the police car which just enough room for me to scuttle between the two cars and into his car. I didn't want to keep him waiting. I am in enough trouble.

He flips through a few papers on a clip board while he closes out a conversation with another cop on a two-way radio. I am glad he is distracted. It gives me a few moments to catch my breath.

I thought everything was perfect. On one side of the street were huge houses that were set back so far from the road that you could barely see them. On the other side was a golf course bordered by large trees that provided a large dark place, big enough to hide a 1968 Chevy Station Wagon.

Everything was perfect until the loud sounds. Bang! Bang! Bang! It was the bottom of his flashlight hitting against the driver side window in rapid succession. Immediately, I right myself and try to pull up. My hips are frantically banging against the steering wheel as I try to get right with all the might I can muster in the cramped space. The flashlight is now shining its light back and forth across my lap. I am in a panic.

The flashlight goes dark. "Join me in my car right now!" he commands, and mercifully backtracks to the police car. With a slower heartbeat, I am able to get decent. Something doesn't feel right but I think that I am presentable. Jules approaches the same.

I open my car door, place my foot on the ground, then turn facing Jules, and tell her, "I'll be back as soon as I can." Jules nods in consent, still addressing the buttons on her blouse.

He turns off the two-way radio with a quick jab of his finger. Turning to me, he says, "What the hell were you doing?"

"Parking," I respond in a subservient manner. I do not want any argument. I am at his mercy.

"And what about the girl?" is his gruff response.

"She's my girlfriend."

"What are you gonna do if you put her in trouble?"

"I use protection," still subservient.

"Protection, huh." He takes a breath. In that moment, I chance another glance in his direction. He had turned to look out his window. He turns back to me.

"Waddaya say I take you both home to your parents? Would you like that? . . . Heh? Would ya?"

"No, I prefer if you would just take it out on me. It's my car. It's my domicile."

"Oh shit . . . What did I just say," I think to myself, "a little bit of pressure, and I turn into Perry Mason!"

"Ok . . . maybe I just arrest you . . . let her go. You Ok with that?"

"Yeah, sure," helplessly hoping.

"That goes on your record kid. It makes it difficult finding a job when you grow up. You still OK with that?"

I can tell that he's looking at me. He's silent, waiting for me to say something. I can't think of anything. I can't find words. Even if I'm arrested, her parents, everyone, will find out. My head drops. All is lost.

A few seconds of deafening silence lasts forever.

"I tell you what kid, just get back in your car and get the hell outta here. And if I ever catch you in the Village of East Hills again, it's gonna be bad for you. You understand me?"

"Yes sir."

"Get out of my car!"

I'm back in my car in a second. "He's letting us go."

"That's a relief," Jules replies.

I fumble around at my feet, feeling around for my shoes.

"What are you doing?"

"Looking for my shoes."

"Your shoes? . . . You mean, you sat in the police car all this time, in your socks?"

"Yeah. I couldn't keep him waiting. It took me long enough to get presentable. Any longer, and I would've pissed him off." I find a shoe under the gas pedal. With my chest tight against the steering wheel and my hand close to the floor, I slip on the loafer. It's not easy. I discover the second shoe in between the seat and the door.

Jules starts laughing, quiet at first. Then she covers her mouth with her hand as the laughter comes up from down deep.

I wrestle with the second shoe. It wrestles back. I'm taking too much time. I begin to worry about the cop. I gotta get while the gettin's good.

She laughs louder. It's a full belly laugh.

"Shhhh! Please. If he hears us laughing, this whole thing can go south. Please."

It's no use what I say. Her head is back against the headrest. It's a large laugh, and nonstop, broken up occasionally by the words, "Police car" and "socks."

I forget about the second shoe and start the car. I pull back from the police car, make a quick U-turn. I drive away as fast as possible without risking his attention. Jules continues to laugh. My eyes continually search the rearview mirror for his headlights. I make a series of quick right and left turns that should render us invisible, or at least hard for him to follow.

By the time we escape from the Village of East Hills, Jules brings her laughter to the level of a suppressed giggle. My breathing returns to normal.

"That was close," I say, glancing towards her.

Her lips pressed closed, she maintains a respectable silence, for a few moments at least, until, "I can't believe you were talking to that cop for all that time, sitting there in your socks."

Her laughter makes a big comeback.

Exhausted from romance, police, and the getaway, I surrender to her moment. Like a drowning sailor, I give up the ghost and join in her laughter, slow at first, then syncopated with the meter and verse of her joy.

I drop her off, safe at home.

It's the laughter I remember, whenever I remember.

Naked Boys Walking
Looking for Girls
to Play Strip Poker

Skinny dipping is a vocation. One is called.

For most, it will suffice to find a pond, small lake, or reservoir hidden in the pines, or covered by a canopy of elm trees, or entombed by the interlaced quilt of maple leaves.

Perhaps one is a lone walker in the woods, disrobing to enjoy one's solitary splash upon the meniscus of the lone lake. Less is more. Simplify, simplify, simplify whispers the summer breeze. You are, who you are, in the forest.

Or maybe it's a spur of the moment thing with the usual crew of friends and lovers. The sun bears hot upon the back of your neck. Jeans, instead of shorts, remind you of how hot and sticky summer gets in this part of the country. All it takes is one brave girl. No one is sure if it is the laughter or the scream that you hear first. There is no denying that the sight of one hot, crazy, maiden making a naked mad dash for the pond is one's favorite box of eye candy. You, he, she, they follow suit, screaming, laughing, splashing into one big happy pond of irreverent joy.

It happens. No one gets hurt. All live to dip another day.

Then there are the aficionados who seek out the right balance of trespassing, danger, and the cold fresh dive into private pools. Such are the souls of Owen and myself.

We start with affluent neighborhoods because that's where the best pools are found. Extra points if the pool is near a police precinct or borders country club grounds routinely patrolled by local deputies or Pinkertons. A diving board high enough to warrant one large splash or the challenge of racking up several dives with minimal splash enhances the Olympic scoring of the event. The evening becomes a trifecta if the people are at home with lights on and their silhouettes visible in first floor windows.

It's not for everybody but, we've done it.

One summer night, the fellas and I find ourselves in a house in the Hamptons, the chic summer neighborhood on the southern fork of Long Island. It's a small one-floor house of modestly proportioned rooms, including two bedrooms. A friend of a friend's parents owns the house. All but one of my friends either know him only in passing, or not at all. He is at the house, making new friends.

The house is set back far from any road. It is in the middle of nowhere. The traditional trappings of the Hamptons be far, far away, in another space and time. Our posse drinks to excess for no purpose other than simple camaraderie.

At some point late in the evening, Owen and I get the calling to dip.

It is late in the evening. We are three sheets to the wind. A thunderbolt renders that which is obscure but obvious to the inebriated consciousness: why wait to get naked after you find the pool?

Let's go boldly into that night!

Resplendent in our birthday suits, we embark down a small, dirt road in pursuit of a pool. After all, this is the Hamptons. A pool cannot be far off.

Oblivious to the elements and our precarious exposure, we invoke the great conversations of the ages as in a great Greek odyssey. We progress step by step, our fate closer to that of the Greek tragedy than that of the comedy in our heads.

Fifteen minutes down the road, the sighting of a small country house interrupts our discourse on the purpose and meaning of life. Unfortunately, there is no pool. However, great men of genius often look beyond the obvious, especially when under the influence of greater spirits. It becomes entirely plausible that there could be girls in this house playing strip poker. Nature abhors a vacuum. We approach the house with sugar plums and more prurient images dancing in our heads.

Suddenly, a car comes out of nowhere and turns into the dirt driveway of the house. This has a sobering effect. As the car proceeds up the driveway, the headlights illuminate the buttocks of two errant travelers making haste into the forest.

We reach home base. No pool. No girls. Out of breath. We crash and burn into the two respective beds of the two small bedrooms in the house of a friend of a friend. Morning brings headaches and remorse but a scattered memory of a night well spent in the pursuit of frivolity.

Tis a far, far better thing to dip then to never dip at all; even when there is no dip at all but for two drunken dips.

Bees Best Be
Not at The Beach

I wake to a rosy-fingered dawn. A brief rain at first light exposes a rainbow in the sky. It has no clear beginning nor any discernible end. The colors appear like a marching band, all in order, traversing the sky in a brigade. The rainbow holds out promise, then disappears behind a brief, dense rain.

I crawl out of bed. My soul finds the day wanting. Something in my soul grows through the dawn. An errant seed comes into bloom. Saturday is restless. The day needs filling. Affection, confidences, great conversations hold less truck this day. I call the attractive barfly who chats me up every other Friday night at a pub filled with underage teenagers.

We walk from the parking lot onto the pure white sand of the ocean beach at noon. Tall grasses decorate the sand dunes that serve as a bulwark against the surf and its relentless attack on the shore.

The horizon holds up the deepest blue canvas.

Today, there are bees among the tall grasses, flitting from one blade to another in search of a flower's nectar. Long grass has no flower. The bees' whereabouts and the day's toil offer no hope of honey for workers and queen. It is a dangerous neighborhood for bees. The cool ocean breeze precludes safe passage back to the hive. These bees will not dance, nor tap out the distance and direction back to the tall grasses, nor receive a warm welcome from fellow workers.

They are lost.

No stray sunbeam enlightens their minds as to their plight. No thermal rises from sand to lift them above their immediate pursuit and return them back to their station. They soldier on in their duty. At least there is a nobility in their quest, their light brigade.

Not so for those who engage in their own folly, trying to skirt the just, and steal the gratuitous and undeserved.

It's a brief walk on the beach. We talk of nothing memorable, just passing the time. It's a chilly April day. The wind is hard. My jacket zipped, my hands stuffed into the pockets of my jeans, we leave by way we came. Passing over the dunes, I notice the bees are no longer flying or buzzing about the tall grass of the sand dunes. Instead the bees are in the sand, crawling or dead.

Jules, Pat, and other girlfriends are coincidentally at the beach that same day. Pat sees me leaving. "Is that Bob," she asks, "and who is that with him?"

"I don't know," Jules says as the breath escapes her.

Bees best be not at the beach.

．　．　．

"I was at the beach on Saturday and I saw you with someone. Do you want to tell me about it?" she asks.

"Of course," he says. "It didn't mean anything." He is thinking about the barfly, the quick ride to the beach, a short walk on the beach and dropping her off at her home. There was a kiss goodbye and a brief pass of his hand across her sweater. He tells her everything except about the brief trespass of the sweater.

He is honest, nothing, almost nothing to hide.

He forgets recent answers to her recent questions. If she does, what will be left . . . left to hold him? Where will we go from there? He forgets about the description of the house with the white picket fence and children running in the yard.

"I don't know why I did it. She doesn't mean anything to me. When I dropped her off and rode away, I said to myself, 'Why did I do that?' I would rather spend time with you." His look and tone are sincere. He doesn't know any better.

He doesn't see the hurt, the lie without words. 'It's been only a short time, and this?' she thinks. Her eyes water but he can't see it as he stares at the ground. He only wants it all to go away, to be over, as if it never happened. He fidgets.

"Are we alright?" he asks.

He doesn't hear the answer in her silence. He disappoints. He is found wanting. He insists to himself that it was nothing, a minor indiscretion.

He rises to leave.

Only a fool believes.

.   .   .

I drove my car over to her house in the middle of the day. It was a brief phone call. She wants to see me. She had something to talk about. It's been a week since our last conversation.

I do not remember exactly what, or how she says it. I only recall walking out through the door at the end of the brief, dark hallway leading from the small TV room. When the sun hits my face as I stand in the backyard, I realize that it's over. She ended it. And furthermore, she tells me that she has decided to take up with Peter, a recent and, now ex-friend of mine.

It's all a blur and a shock.

So it goes for a fool and his folly.

.   .   .

Five weeks later, a sibling calls me to the phone, "It's for you."

"Hi," comes a tentative voice from the phone. It was a short phone conversation. Of course, I take her back. She is beautiful, gentle and kind.

The summer becomes precious in its austerity. Each day brings us closer to the end of my high school world and the beginning of college.

In those early days of college, her memory comforts me. One evening each week, I call from the public telephone in the dorm foyer with a pocketful of quarters. I miss her.

One day at the cafeteria, I step up to the sandwich bar with its small containers of sandwich meats, cheeses, jelly and peanut butter. A fly lands on the peanut butter. It can't escape. I quickly grab a knife, cover it over with peanut butter, then return to my seat.

My roommates love the story. I am with my people.

Just Stupid

Binghamton is only an hour bus ride from Oneonta. I step off the bus and walk into the bus depot, a dirty place. It's raining outside, a typical winter day in upstate New York. The area had great expectations back in the day. But airlines supersede railroads and the future flies over upstate New York and has yet to return. I wait for the sight of Peter's red Ford Mustang, an older version Mustang, but it's still cool and a car is always better than no car.

Peter and I are back on relatively friendly terms and I need something to do this weekend.

The Mustang pulls up to the curb. I hop in the passenger side.

A few inches smaller than me and skinnier than most people, Peter greets me with a big smile. There's no handshake since he has the ever-present cigarette in his right hand. As a late comer to our high school crowd, he never was into sports but he is smart with a quick, irreverent wit. He often has everyone in stitches, especially after he passes around funny cigarettes for everyone's taking.

"No bag or anything?" Peter inquires.

"Nah. It's only a 24-hour trip."

"Suit yourself. I have to drop you off at Jack's dorm for a few minutes while I run an errand," he says.

"No problem. I was hoping to see Jack while I was here."

We exchange notes on our respective freshman years. No big news. He pulls to the curb in front of a campus dorm.

"Jack's in room 212. I'll pick you up in an hour and we'll do dinner at my dining hall," he says.

"Fine. See you soon. Honk or scream and I'll come running."

He pulls away from the curb. The Mustang disappears around a bend spewing dark exhaust like coughs from a weary old man.

I knock on the door of the second-floor dorm room. The door opens. It's Jack, all six feet of him, still thin and wiry but with a bushy beard. College looks good on him. After a handshake and a hearty embrace, I am in the study of his quad, a two-bedroom dorm room. Decorations are sparse but the room's clean. We sit down and catch up on the doings of all our high school friends who are, like us, at this midpoint in our freshman year.

"Peter's getting it together with some girl on campus," he volunteers. "She's not bad looking. He may be the first one of us to score at college," he mutters with the indifference unique to the adolescent male.

"Great," I respond. But I'm thinking, "Why shouldn't I be the first to get a notch on my belt?" thoughtless of the girlfriend at home. I can't help but note the coldness in my last thought. I shrug it off and put it out of my mind. I am only here to catch up with a few friends and have a few beers before returning to Oneonta.

Peter's back. Jack and I pack ourselves into the Mustang.

"We'll do dinner and head over to Rich's dorm," Peter says. "There's a party there." Rich is an acquaintance from high school, now elevated to friend status since we share upstate New York.

A few hours and too many beers later, I find myself in a serious lip-lock with Peter's new girlfriend. I can't recall the build up to this moment, only that it is happening and I initiated it. She holds nothing back in her response but I am a stranger in a strange land without quarters.

The girl and I part that evening on friendly terms.

The next morning, Peter drives me to the bus depot. There is no conversation. He is stone faced. I exit the car, close the door and before I can turn to initiate a farewell through the window, the Mustang roars off.

The Girl, Interrupted

The brilliancy of the morning star eclipses all other light and guides her step off the bus as she enters the world of my small college town. I take her small backpack, sling it onto my back, slipping one arm through its straps. We walk east, down Main Street towards the college bus stop, making small talk about her trip.

One does not think of the dying, the fall from grace, the chipping away of one's soul. Nor the moment after, when everything will be different. I do not realize that what is done cannot be undone.

There was glory and joy the first time that love fell upon me like a waterfall, my lover's face, the reflection of boy she loves. A shallow hubris proceeds me now, one step at a time towards the denigration of that special gift and a commitment to cherish and protect it.

I am unaware of the power of demons to slip quietly and unnoticed into the soul. I am not familiar with their power to wait patiently, to align themselves with the rhythm and cadence of a life. Like a fair-weather friend, they share in my joys and sorrows and affix themselves with whispers and false promises to my heart and mind.

Unaware, I walk beside myself paying lip service to the hole in my soul and the first love that filled it. College parties, greater freedom and a false sense of invisibility that comes from being away from home give greater voice to demons and their subtle, relentless whisper that life has a little bit more to offer, and a little more has to be a little bit better.

It begins with a harmless visit to see Peter. Drinking, smoking, and ultimately rolling in the grass with a girl, Peter's girl, our arms embraced, lips locked.

She calls a couple of weeks later and suggests a visit. I agree. She steps off the bus this Saturday morning into my weekend, changing my life forever.

The day passes with walks across campus, coffee and conversation.

For lunch, we pull up chairs at a table in a campus cafeteria, relieving a friend, coincidentally named Peter, of his solitude. We notice that we all chose the fried fish-balls for our lunch.

"That's great," says my new friend du jour, "until you think of all those poor, castrated fish that gave their all for our lunch."

Peter's jaw drops slightly and quickly turns into a smile to match a wild look in his eyes. "Yes," he says, "we must always be mindful of the misbegotten."

Laughter and light banter follow.

Ultimately, the morning star disappears. Angels fall from heaven. Dark covers the sky as the day ends in my dorm room. She rises from the chair in the study and enters my bedroom alone. I am left in the company of my two quad-mates who share the other double room; my roommate is conveniently away for the weekend.

"Well, she's in there," one says.

I remain in my chair, reluctant to start in motion the steps that will lead to the act that would fulfill the purpose of the visit. The last vestige of decency and loyalty within me begs me to call it off, to enter the bedroom and sit on the floor and explain that I have a girlfriend and that I am a creep to have led her on this way. But I don't have the courage for the truth. I rise cowardly from the chair and enter my bedroom.

It is only the thin veneer of latex that feigns any sense of affection or decency. I roll off and away from her. She feels the truth.

My soul freefalls to the staccato pulse of a flickering, invisible strobe. I am a little bit more dead to myself but I do not know it. Demons never let you know. She hates me. I hate myself.

Sunday morning at the bus depot, winter makes a comeback. Trash decorates the floors and piles up against the walls that know not the comfort of pictures or posters, nor windows the touch of drapes or upholstery. She purchases her ticket.

"There's no need for you to wait", she says coldly.

"I'll see you off," I say with a fallow sense of chivalry.

The bus comes. She boards without salutation. I walk back to campus. My world shatters.

. . .

A car races along the highway in late afternoon, through winding roads onto a tree lined street into the dark of a winter rain. The Mustang pulls up the driveway towards an upscale house with red brick exterior and full-grown trees in the front yard. Peter exits the car, closing the car door with a loud bang, he rushes to the dark, wooden front door protected by a canopy and light. He pounds a hard and hurried knock. She is home alone. She opens the door in a casual, unhurried manner of those whose world is secure and intact.

The two figures retreat to the living room, furnished in a casual and understated elegance. She sits in a comfortable living room chair; he pulls up a more austere wooden chair and plants it directly across from her. Peter sits, takes one breath and begins to talk quickly with emphatic, exaggerated hand motions, intermittently feigning compassion and understanding. After a few moments, she rises and escorts him to the door. He stops on the inside of the door and faces her. She places a hand on his chest, looks him in the eyes and gives him a farewell kiss on the cheek, her hand motioning him towards the front door, touching and falling from his back as he exits into the rainy night.

She closes the door with one hand on the doorknob and one hand gently pushing the upper part of the door. She rests her head upon the back of her hand that remains upon the door. There is the sound of a car door closing, the start of a car motor and that of a car disappearing down the road into the dark. She feels the cold damp of an unforgiving night as her shoulders tremble slightly. She heads off a slow soft sob emanating from within her with a deep breath. The world is suddenly cold, sparse and unwelcoming.

She swears to herself that this will not make her cry. She holds her head up as if to brace herself against the night. She turns with a slow steady walk to the stairs behind her. She places her hand on the dark cherry wood bannister, pausing for a deep breath. She walks slowly up the stairs, grateful for the softness of the carpet that provides a little cushion in a house that is now colder. Turning at the landing, she completes the last few steps to the second floor, walking into her bedroom. She lays down upon the bed, curling up into a fetal position. She pulls the blankets to her face but it only reminds her of him, once lying in this bed on top of the covers laughing, cuddling, rolling to and fro with her. The bed no longer offers refuge. She cries quietly, the song of a heart looking for shelter or at least escape from warm things that may have a hint of him.

She rises from the bed and walks away, enters the hall bathroom, full of white, cold tiles. She settles herself on the tile floor, back against an empty bathtub, knees up close against arms tucked against her breasts with hands clasped under her chin. The chill of the tile and porcelain slows her heart and offers a numbness, a nominal defense from the outside world.

The demons come. She wonders why. Was not her all enough? Was there something lacking? Was the other woman special . . . more beautiful . . . possessing talents that she did not . . . what made him look away . . . she gave her all . . . and now she is alone. She is afraid of breaking, of crying. The slight numbing from cold offers small comfort and less protection.

She is grateful for good parents, loving siblings, and a best friend that she will see tomorrow or maybe the next day. She will eventually meet him, to tell him that she knows what he does not tell her. She will end it. But for now, she seeks only a cold embrace so that she can feel a little less, to keep the dark at bay. Her dreams of loving the boy, a white picket fence, a home, and children running in the yard become distant and fade. All that is, is memory. She knows what she has to do tomorrow, or the day after, or the next day. But tonight, is for sorrow, the last rite for a failed future.

.   .   .

The first true love of my life picks me up at the bus station at the end of the school year. She knows. She gives me my walking papers.

Demons love truth and justice applied at the right time and in the right measure. Truth shatters worlds, aiding and abetting the demon's vocation of misery and suffering. My truth has them dancing through the summer and into the New Year.

We join together at a later date. We embrace. We love again. But we walk with demons. They escort us to the supermarket. They sit between us at the movies. They never cease to remind us of what we are not now. They make conversations with others than ourselves, more interesting and entertaining.

"We are both just looking for something better to come along," she's says at the end of the summer and leaves for her sophomore year.

. . .

Thanksgiving week is always cold on Long Island. The Long Island Sound to the north and the Atlantic Ocean on the southern shore make for a sure carry of moisture in the air that bites the skin. This night harbors a cold, bitter rain.

Even the trees exude a foul mood. Leaves made heavy by the November rain give a sarcastic applause as they clap themselves together, driven by an indifferent wind. Trees bow their greeting to a son whom they find shallow and wanting.

I pull my coat closer, a navy-blue overcoat that I picked up from an upstate Goodwill shop. It serves its purpose and keeps me warm and dry down to my knees. There is no relief for my feet in high white Converse All Stars well past their prime.

I know it's over. I called her dorm room a month ago, late on a Saturday night. She recognized me at "Hi." She's not a good liar. She's fumbles with the phone and her words. I can all but see him.

Like most patrons, I enter the bar from the side-street door. The pool table and the pub are in full swing. The light in the back room hangs precariously over the pool table. I turn into the darkness of the bar where she greets me.

"We have to talk," she says. We claim two chairs at a small table. Sitting, facing each other, I can't say it.

She delivers the mail, "I found somebody else. I am in love."

I nod. I know her. I believe her.

She reaches across the table and holds my hand. It's a soft, gentle and genuine gesture. We lock eyes. "I hope that we can be friends," she says.

"I have loved you too much to ever be friends with you," I reply. We part, forever.

Carefree Highway

"Indeed, the safest road to Hell is the gradual one—the gentle slope, soft underfoot, without sudden turnings, without milestones, without signposts, ... Your affectionate uncle, Screwtape."

— C.S. Lewis, *The Screwtape Letters*.

It made sense at the time. And Ron agreed, at first. Ron is my college roommate since freshman year. And Ron has nice hair—long, thick, straight, midnight black hair. On more than one occasion, when he was being quiet and apart from the crowd in a pub, a girl would tell him that he has beautiful hair. Ron would look up, smile, and thank her. Ron is also very funny. He can take over a whole room with funny. But that is a different story in another book. This is the story of a road less travelled, the story of a carefree highway.

The bars close at 2 o'clock in the morning on Saturday night. Our blood alcohol level protects us from winter's cold. Ron and I begin the walk back to the house from the downtown bars. It is as simple as seeing a road sign pointing in the direction to Binghamton. This inspires me to suggest that we hitchhike to Binghamton. Ron agrees wholeheartedly in the spirit of a stupor. With a steady stream of drunk drivers heading home at 2 AM, our first ride comes quickly. The second ride takes longer. A lone stoner picks up and drops us off on the outskirts of Bainbridge, about twenty miles short of Binghamton where we hope to hook up with friends.

Car traffic becomes sparse around three AM. We walk. And walk. And walk some more. The sky is pitch black. The cold is merciless.

I bury my hands in my winter coat and hold it tight. Ron does likewise. As the alcohol wears off, it dawns on us that this is less than fun. Apart from complaining about the cold, Ron becomes distant and none too happy with me and my bright ideas. We walk the night in silence, alone with our thoughts.

At the end of last semester, I said goodbye to my new girlfriend at JFK airport with an embrace of sweet sorrow. She was off to study abroad for the Spring semester. A pale complexion amidst natural platinum blond tresses, she practices indifference in greetings and goodbyes. She staves off the reproaches of airport security for quick passage to her gate. She is her own person, a young woman in sync with her times. It was easy to fall in like with her. She is intelligent, witty and irreverent.

"Ok. Take care of yourself. Write. Write often. And don't forget me," she says, half ordering and half in jest.

I can't help but smile. She has a place in my heart. She kept it beating after the break-up. Despite all her good qualities, she cannot keep me from turning back the pages to the times I loved best.

She boards the plane. I let the Atlantic Ocean and time speak for me in lieu of the truth. As a woman of character, she deserves the truth. I take my signature cowardly exit.

The relentless cold shocks me back into the present. We have no choice but to keep walking. The night, like the forest and fields on both sides of the road, goes on forever.

My mind wanders back to where I pick up the pieces of this dream shattered night. Love comes again with an impish smile, olive skin, bright brown eyes that are alive as the sun, and can rise like the wind into a temper or an embrace. She is like a chestnut mare, for love of the ride, if you don't mind jumping off high cliffs into pools of shallow water. She expects to float. She likes boys like I like girls.

We are in the new library. I was simply paying the price for her company. She needs a book on the upper floor. I press the elevator button for the third floor and then pull the emergency button. Suspended between floors, I grabbed her derriere and pull her up, her hips rest on mine, back pressed to the wall. Her head falls back with laughter. She wraps her legs around my waist. She lets out a muffled shriek of joy.

We kiss to unbridled fun. Her skin is soft and her breasts full and free against my chest. I pin her to the wall with my hips and reach down to her jeans.

She laughs harder and exposes a long slender neck. I kiss the neck, her face, her lips while my hands work overtime on her jeans.

"You're kidding!" she exclaims between laughs and kisses "I would love to but I have to lay flat to take off these jeans, and it takes forever to put them back on."

My heartbeat slows. It would be hard to explain this "emergency" to a small troupe of firefighters once the elevator doors open. I am a beaten man. I lower her to the ground, push the emergency button with resignation. We exit onto the third floor with a few students waiting to board the elevator, none the wiser. "My kingdom for a miniskirt!" I whisper under my breath. She laughs an encore.

Eventually, she tenders me my papers, lights up a smoke and dismisses me as her distraction du jour. It doesn't bother me. She was fun. This thing that I call living now, is all about being satisfied. And if it breaks for the good, or for the bad, I know that I got no one else to blame.

Dawn breaks on our backcountry highway. It's still freezing cold but we welcome the sun like an old friend. We have no idea how far we are in terms of miles or hours from our destination. It is only desperation that brings us to approach a farmhouse for assistance.

Ron and I, two long-haired, ragged, strangers walk up a dirt driveway about the length of a football field and make a modest knock on the front door. It is only a little bit past dawn. A middle-aged woman of considerable heft, hidden by an apron, opens the door and to our surprise, invites us inside. From the dining room to our right, three young men the size of Division One college football players and their father greet us with a hearty hello. Scrambled eggs, sausage, ham and sliced homemade bread decorate the table. Two scrawny longhair college bumpkins pose no threat to this household.

We explain our plight and ask for assistance. They explain that they are about to start their workday but if we keep walking down the highway, we should get a ride since a lot of cars will be commuting to Binghamton.

We walk on. Quiet remains between us. The journey that began in the wee hours in the morning still holds us captive. Sobriety intrudes on our morning and invites his companion, hangover, to share the morning with us. Ultimately, God smiles. A recent graduate from SUNY picks us up and drops us off on his way to work at the local bus depot in downtown Binghamton.

Turning up at our house in Oneonta sometime in the afternoon, our housemates express their concern about our absence. "We had no idea where you were all night. We wouldn't put anything past either of you. Ron would jump off a building to make Bob laugh. And when Ron goes splat on the ground, Bob would laugh," they said. Ron and I laugh.

.   .   .

Sometime thereafter, high, elegant, almost haughty cheekbones draw my attention to the big, deep pair of brown eyes that suggest the ruin of many a poor boy. She licks each of my fingers resting on her shoulder. Then comes noise of the apartment door opening, footsteps in the kitchen. "That's my boyfriend," she whispers in my ear.

Imbued with the wisdom of a naked man, I do nothing.

He enters the dark room and sits calmly on the bed. Careful not to harm her, he rests his hand gently on my thigh. She raises up from the bed, bent at the waist, with the sheet pulled up over her breasts. "I'm with someone," she says softly, "please step outside." He withdraws to the kitchen.

"You should leave," she says to me in the same soft voice. "Sorry," she adds. At this point, I set the world's record for getting dressed.

I pass by the boyfriend in the kitchen, relieved that I have a few inches on him. He is absent an angry face. I offer up a nod in passing and make my exit. Downstairs on the street, I meet a bracing, cold burst of upstate winter air. Another night, another long walk in the cold under a dark sky. Only this time I am alone. I walk home to a cold, one room apartment. I am satisfied with it, knowing I got no one left to blame.

.   .   .

It's a small bedroom like any other in a small single apartment in this small bucolic college town. Posters on the wall, faux flowers on her dresser, and a peaceful, easy feeling from a young woman who knows herself.

I am currently a refugee from an office in New York City that has a thousand people at a thousand desks, tethered to a thousand phones, chasing a margin above minimum wage in a soulless job.

We marry our love for comfort and fun. We share dreams. We talk of bullfights in Madrid, running with the bulls in Pamplona, Greek island beaches and all that beckons. Our todays suffice as long as tomorrows fill with adventure.

Looking out her window as the evening turns to night and the room feels especially warm, I whisper, "If I could be anyplace in the world right now, I would choose to be here." The words hold true for a moment.

She is honest. She always tells the truth to her hometown boyfriend. They talk of marriage. But only after she finishes being free. He loves her. He always accepts her truth.

Comes the day when the boyfriend tires of forgiveness. My next visit becomes her last truth to him. He says good-bye to her over the phone. She tells me of the breakup. She thinks that he was the one for her, to have and to hold. I listen but I have no truck for tears, no legal tender to compensate her for regret. My soul is long spent on a pocket full of promises.

I begin to feel like a cartoon character in a cartoon graveyard. In my mind's eye, I see myself sitting like the puppet, Pinocchio—smoking cigars, drinking beer, playing pool, hanging out with jack-asses, and a day at a time, drowning in lost.

I can only but help bounce the last check of her freedom.

. . .

I fall in love for a night again, and again, until there is no light left in August and I wake in a different state . . . from my head down to my shoes.

Short of The Promised Land

The natural food coop occupies the furthest fringe of the northern campus which is a substantial bus ride to the main campus in Ann Arbor. It is here that alley cats congregate, held together by a desire for sustenance without toxins.

Her eyes are big and dark, sunk behind cheekbones and with a dark rouge patina surrounding each one. You get the feeling that she cries a lot, or she constantly reels from the memories of being picked last, or from being passed over altogether. She is thin and wiry. She reminds me of a cat that must earn or scrummage for her fare every day. Nights bring rest. Morning sun is rarely welcome.

Today, at this moment, she is excited. The eyes are wide open. The lips move in quick enunciation.

"And I just happened upon her diary. Out of nowhere, it falls into my lap. I opened it. I was startled to see her words. Someone was like me. She has the same feelings. I don't know if it was an epiphany or simply relief."

She pauses. I smile. We are on the bus ride to the main campus. We share the early phase of friendship. Although we talk in subdued tones, we are oblivious to the other riders. We share the camaraderie of those on the margin.

We boarded the bus at the stop for us, the food co-op.

Her lover, an older woman, sees her off with a kiss and returns to their abode filled with natural foods. Her lover walks slowly and without impediment. Only her lover's shoulders hint at the weariness, aware of a precarious date with the world when they will marry their fortunes together. Today, they bury it all in a kiss.

She insists on being true to herself. Today is free of classes and appointments. She focuses only on the meal, prepared with promises of health and well-being. They will share it in the evening. Tonight, they will sleep the sleep of lovers.

We empty from the bus at the center of campus. We exchange our goodbyes. She scurries across the quad, moving quickly and skillfully against the tide of other students. She is feral versus their congeniality. She enters the library. She knows what she wants and what she needs to do that day. She will skip lunch, drink a lot of coffee and return on the bus come dark.

My day is like hers, only I am more alone.

I find my way to the business school cafeteria. It is a spartan place, resplendent in beige tile and linoleum flooring. A hardboiled egg and a cup of tea for breakfast, then on to accounting and human resources classes. It's a long way from Blake, Hemingway and Faulkner, but recessions do that to you.

At the end of the day, I return to the north campus. I have my own bed in a double that I share with a roommate. There is a third student who has a single room with whom we share a study room.

But this evening, I return again to the co-op where I have dinner in a makeshift dining room. I lay claim to some soup and vegetables. A woman who is unsure of the day and the time, offers her room to me for the night. It's not the first time. We are not lovers, only bedfellows.

It's almost evening. There should be some residual daylight in her room but there isn't. There never is. I don't look for the reason—a building or a tree, shading the window. Daylight is simply unwelcome. It is an older student room, plain and functional with a single bed, closet and small chest of drawers. A few small cactuses serve as decorative plant life, catching the meager light and moisture afforded in this netherworld.

She has a face unspoiled by beauty. She has a name but we never use each other's names. She doesn't share memories. Over time, she allows a ray of light upon the unborn whom she ushered to another space and time and the visits to doctors that protect her from the gifts of men with no faces.

We become lovers in a night that has no exit door. I slip into dream-shattered sleep. I wake, restless, my throat parched. I leave the room and step into the night.

I walk forward to keep my demons at bay. They are legion and they abound with bad intent. Like stray dogs tied to a spike, they leap towards me in my mind's eye; their faces shapeshift into men's faces lost in agony. Only their chains and the spike keep them from consuming me.

The occasional star flickers against the night like an electric light reaching the end of its life. The voices grow louder. Theirs is to laugh, mine to despair.

A small creek bars my path. The whisper that comes up from the clean rushing water over small rocks, beckons me to stop. I sit in the company of a boulder, my counselor and confessor. Clouds cover all stars. The far shore but for a few steps into dark water, holds me at bay.

My offering consists of a few drops of sentiment for all that will be green in the dawn's light. The day holds no promise for me. I spent the rosy finger dawns of my past.

I walk a sparse path back to her room in darkness. My feet can't feel to step but this is the path of my own making. The stones call out and mock me for my past and futile attempts at redemption.

I return from where I came. I retreat to her bed. Her breathing is like the rhythmic remnant of a mountain stream pulsing slowly forward, only to expire onto an arid plain of quiet desperation. Staring at the ceiling, I listen to my breath, wishing it would cease.

I rise and quietly leave the room and walk away. Only by the grace of a benevolent deity, I know not how cold is this night nor distant the dawn.

The Reunion

I park the car on the suburban street that always has enough space for the occasional barbecue or get-together like today, a reunion of those from the neighborhood who cohabitated in all forms together as a group except for the prurient kind which we did alone in couples and left unsaid to protect and share something special in teenage years which would get us in trouble with parents, priests, brothers, nuns who were in charge of our souls, and blessed or cursed with the task of escorting us, individually and corporately, into the promised land which must resemble the suburbs in some way because in this pastoral landscape all are equal as evidenced by the pretty little houses with pretty little the patches of green lawn, and the short cement walk leading up to the three steps that bring one up to the front door, with or without wrought iron railings, which always opens once one presses the small, opaque, circular doorbell which summons the host who always leans forward, off balance just a bit, holding the screen door open so that you can squeeze one at a time into the house that has the living room on the right and a dining room on the left that leads into the kitchen where you can leave the little tidbit of finger food that the host will put either on the dining room table or the picnic table on the back porch which in this case is elevated above the ground courtesy of dark brown wood decking that makes the back porch even with the above-ground outdoor pool so that children, especially my three daughters, can jump directly from the back deck into the water, whose splashes infringe upon the beer-pong game to the left of the pool, in full swing complete with an intergenerational game of fathers versus sons, the fathers patiently launching each toss of the ping pong ball, the first bounce being on this side of the net which carefully and seemingly in slow-motion clears the small net with a high jump to hopefully land in a cup, partially filled with beer for purposes of stabilization, and should the ping pong ball land in a cup, arms are raised in jubilation at the prospect of the other team drinking to excess which in this situation, is made up of the sons and their friends who mostly know each other from high school and college lacrosse teams which is made evident by the their trim waists rising up into broad shoulders carried upon strong backs ripped with muscles under tee shirts, from long hours of practices, push-ups and running up and down, a 100 yard field wielding sticks with small nets made for catching, holding and throwing a small hard ball, so hard that each player must wear the extra protection that only catchers wore in Little League to save the family jewels from the most inglorious of fates, the writhing and crying, and the crying and writhing that never seems to end but can go way in an instant if the eye catches the shape of something soft, with curves that immediately draws one's eye in for a closer look at that which captures all men's souls and makes irrelevant the pain and the boredom of the work-a-day world just so long as he can come home to the prospect of holding one so soft, gentle and kind that it novates all thoughts of the sweating, toiling, competing and just being manly for no other reason than to get the girl which makes it all make sense and worthwhile in his stumbling, bumbling efforts towards a home that this man builds for that girl, that woman, who will direct his days and educate him about the finer things that justifies his self to his day, his life and, to his God, and that is one of the reasons that I come to this house, on this block, in this town, to see, and perhaps to talk, to that girl who first causes me to be woke.

It is a high school reunion of sorts, for the group of men and women that share a common neighborhood and their youthful years. Most attended same-sex Catholic high schools and a few went to local public high schools.

Elizabeth, my spouse of almost twenty years, a slim, beautiful, brunette, possessed of a congenial spirit and a blessedly comfortable way with herself and strangers, enters the backyard with me and our girls. The twins are thirteen and the youngest, the boss, is ten years of age.

The men sport a little grey around their temples and a few share a larger belt size indicative of a lifestyle a bit more corpulent than that of their parents. All the men turn fifty years of age this calendar year, the impetus for the reunion, and most of the female alumnus follow a year behind.

The afternoon sun shines bright upon family, food, and friendship.

Sometime later, she arrives with her husband. They receive a hearty welcome. They are in the company of friends.

I am oddly alert to her presence through the afternoon. We have not spoken for almost thirty years. I never spoke to anyone about the end of our affair. It's as if I stuffed it all in a pirate's chest, tied it up with a rope and threw it overboard. It sunk deep and never saw the light of day again.

By mid-afternoon, my old crew and I are waist-high into stories of being chased by the cops, being caught by the cops, ditching the cops— sometimes on foot, sometimes in cars. Nothing can bring back those hours of fast cars and brave bar fights but we find camaraderie in the bonds that tie us together. Of course, the cars get faster and our driving skills sharper, and the police more helpless as we recall the good fight against the powers that be.

In the midst of this happy banter, I hear her voice happily exclaim, "You have three children!" I turn my head to see her by my girls in the pool. I sense a connection between us today, perhaps a nervous anticipation of meeting again after such a long time. Or maybe, it's just me.

Sometime later, I am reveling in old stories with Pat, the high school best friend. I think to myself, "Why can't I talk to her like this?"

Taking off with the grace and couth of a Saint Bernard traipsing through knee-deep snow drifts, I pounce upon her alone at the edge of a dining room table filled with finger food. Unfortunately, my timing is syncopated with a lesser friend from high school who makes for a threesome that becomes a bit awkward.

Jules and I make nice-nice with her until the third party moves on. We are left with a brief social hangover and the space between us.

"How's Peter," she offers up in an attempt at casual conversation.

It hits a nerve. "I never understood that, you and Peter," which I offer up with a side of disdain.

Instantly, a voice inside my head screams at me, "What the hell did you just say?" In a nanosecond, I give myself 40 mental lashes for being an insufferable geek.

She is laughing. I take brief comfort in her laugh but the laugh lasts too long. I screwed up. She tries to hide the nervous.

"Don't mention anything that even hints of your past relationship," advises the voice in back of my head.

"How's your brother Steven?" I offer up a lifeline to a safer subject to cover over my faux pas.

"Steven's going through a divorce at the moment," she responds.

"Mayday! Mayday! You're going down!" screams the guy in the back of my head.

"Keep eye contact," my internal counselor advises me. "Don't you dare look down at her shoes!"

"Oh, I'm sure it's her fault," I offer up in a sympathetic tone, keeping eye contact.

"Yes, thank you. I think so too," she responds.

We keep the conversation going with nominal chatter. I am drowning in awkward.

It is subtle and in slow-motion as if some angel gives me a slight push from behind. My panic ebbs, the moment grants me a look into her eyes. A slight current goes through me . . . 'Ohmygodlookhowgentleandsensitivesheis'.

The next instant arrives to find her at the tail end of polite conversation. There is a brief pause. My mind races for a word, a phrase to offer up in conversation. It doesn't come. I am no help to her.

She fills the space with another comment, offering a lifeline to me.

I'm done. I crash. I burn. I can only excuse myself and withdraw.

Exhausted and embarrassed from my lack of presence and conversation, I seek refuge in an aluminum chair by the pool. Someone asks a question of me and my response is quick and overtly rushed.

"Breathe," I tell myself, "just breathe."

I eventually resettle into the warm comradery of old friends. The time to leave arrives. Elizabeth and I pack the three kids into the car and head for home.

At home, Elizabeth asks of my talk with Jules.

"I got nervous and blew it," I said.

"Don't worry, that just means that you'll be relaxed next time."

Tomorrow morning, at church for Sunday services, I am going through the motions. I am unsettled from a poor night's sleep. In a spot of time between sitting in the pew and kneeling, a prayer escapes from my soul to heaven, "Leave me alone. I am happy now."

More of a plea than a prayer.

Monday, Monday

Next morning, I am in that space between dreams and wakefulness, where angels sometimes dwell. I slept well. It rises up naturally, like a warm wind carried from the deep ocean, over the waves, onto the shore, to comfort the child digging a hole in the white sand. The child lifts his head and peers out to welcome the genius of the deep.

"I love her" comes a gentle voice within, offering testimony to a love lost.

My eyes open. I wake calmly onto this dawn. As my heart unfolds a love letter from remembrances of things past, I look upon the countenance of my sleeping spouse who is no less beautiful in the light of the morning sun and I exhale a breath of relief and contentment.

After scrambled eggs and toast I gather wallet, keys and a scattered mess of manila folders in anticipation of the work week.

Riding to work, the early sun warms the cab of my car. The pirate's chest of memories rises to the surface and bursts open. My ride fills with sentiment from my first love lost. It is palpable. It washes over me in waves. I can't stop it or chase it away with thoughts of the upcoming work day.

As I drive across the Tappan Zee Bridge like I have done before on a thousand mornings, the crosswind carries the words to me, "He leadeth me to still waters."

I shed a tear at the thought of the Almighty taking time out from the world's troubles to shepherd a lost, broken-hearted, undeserving boy from love's labor lost to the still waters of a beautiful spouse and her warm embrace.

The remembrances of things past have their way with me through-out the next three days. Finally, I insist, "Enough!" to myself. I have to bring the focus back to work lest I fall short in my work-a-day world.

Like children, these memories creep back into the cab of my car and share my ride to and from work over the next three weeks. Afterwards, I gently usher these offspring from my ride. "That's all," I insist as I turn my focus back to the present.

The memories persist, then retire after a few months.

Of Husbands and Wives

There women, Mrs. O'Hara, a mother of ten, Mrs. Traube, a mother of seven, and my mother, Eileen, a mother of seven, sit in three aluminum lawn chairs, in various states of repair, talking. Their children, single and married, man the barbecue grill, cooking burgers and franks.

The yard holds them close, arms-length from our garage on one side, bright yellow forsythia immediately to their backs (which masks the rear neighbor's garage resplendent with squirrels and other pests), a singular American Beauty rosebud in the corner, head bowed and unbloodied, a remnant of my sister's 4-H project, and an assortment of green plant life interwoven into the chain-link fence that borders our neighbor's driveway.

"The kids are doing it different these days. Married three years, my daughter is holding off on having children," says Mrs. O'Hara.

Eileen agrees, "Yes, the grandchildren come slower these days. My husband used to say that every time he walked pass by me, I got pregnant."

The threesome share laughter.

"What did we know? Out of high school and married as soon as possible." All nod in smiles and agreement.

"I fell in love with my husband because he was the first person who took me off of Tenth Avenue!" offers up Mrs. Traube.

They all chuckle knowingly, each for reasons unspoken.

"The priests were the only ones who had any college in those days. They talked down to us about what was right and wrong," adds Mrs. O'Hara.

"We were such fools to listen to those priests," declares Eileen.
More chuckling and nodding of heads.

. . .

On one occasion, I envied the Traube family, neighbors from around
the block.

During the age of stickball and tag, they invent zip guns and a new
twist on the game of war. Two small pieces of wood, nailed together to
resemble a pistol with a rubber band nailed to the front makes a zip
gun. When loaded with a small piece of linoleum (leftovers from the
Traube's new basement floor), it begets hours of fun.

The game of war is simple, shoot at each other until all but one player
dies from a linoleum bullet. A hit in the arm or leg counts as a wound
but does not disqualify a player—the penalty being the pain inflicted
by the linoleum bullet which is thin but thick enough to leave a mark
or draw blood. We play until the last man standing wins, or until we
get called for dinner.

We play on the down low because one could conceivably "poke one's
eye out" with a direct hit. Parents abhor this type of fun. The risk is left
unspoken: "What are the odds?"

The zip gun and the game of war have nothing to do with the source
of my envy except that it gave me reason to be on the Traube's block
since they invented the game.

Their father returns home from work carrying big brown supermarket paper bags full of food and snacks. He works for a supermarket
chain. His return brings an immediate halt to the game and all Traube
children run to him to lay claim to his snacks. His smaller children
hug his torso or leg. The older children jump up to grab snacks from
the bags. The Traube family had an unjust number of snacks in the
house—sweet and savory.

Years later, in my twenties, I find myself in church, at Mass—an unusual occurrence at the time.

Word passes among the families: Mr. Traube is not well and they
cannot cure him.

He is in the first pew, directly below the pulpit. He hears the sermon without the aid of a loudspeaker. He sees the priest's expressions. He smiles, nodding his head in affirmation. He has a glow about him. He knows something hidden from the rest of us.

Months later, my mother recounts to me the hour of his passing.

"Mrs. Traube insists on caring for him at home. The sheets are always clean and impeccable, the bed tidy and warm. She gives him the best possible care, far better than anything that he would receive in a hospital, surrounded by those who love him."

"We were all there, all her friends, praying with her, saying the rosary. Mr. Traube is propped up in bed, back against the headrest."

"He is slipping in and out of consciousness until eventually he does not bounce back. His head is down, eyes closed, chin on his chest. Out of nowhere, he raises his right hand to let us know we can stop praying. You can hear a pin drop. He lowers his hand and he's gone. It's as if he was already with the angels."

His love. Her love. Their faith.

Ralph Revisited: Requiem for a Middleweight

"Tell us what time of day defines you. And tell us a little bit about yourselves in the process." She is young, attractive and dressed in a light wrap-around, floor length skirt with a casual top appropriate for a New York City summer day.

We sit on plastic chairs in a circle, in a conference room on the second floor of a theater in Greenwich Village. Half of us are on in years, the other half in grammar school. I listen to the response of my peers in this circle of faces. Many of the older people define themselves by early morning hours, the waking, their coffee time. The younger people confess to varying times throughout the day, as diverse as their neighborhoods.

It's theater. This is an interview. Or better said, we are auditioning for a part in a play. Everyone who wins the audition will write a play with a partner. Each pair of playwrights will share a great gap in their ages, hence the project name, "Mind the Gap," the generation gap. Our plays will be performed in a gathering of friends and family in this theater at the end of the semester.

I didn't think that I would make it this far, to the first round. In my email response, I confess to working for a large corporation for almost forty years, most in corporate finance, a definite buzz-kill. But here I sit in a theater workshop on Bleeker Street, sandwiched between Greenwich Village and the Bowery.

"And what time of day defines you Bob?"

I am stirred from my thoughts. "Eight o'clock" I reply and pause. "Evening" . . . pause . . .

"Summer. When my three daughters, my wife, and I clean up after dinner and head down to a local, roadside, ice cream shack. I get to buy them ice cream."

"Then we meander the sidewalks of our little suburban town, and muse about the summer dresses in shop windows, or soft covered diaries at the stationary store. All this happens around eight o'clock before the girls' bedtime. That's the hour and the moments that best define me."

I step back onto the steamy summer sidewalk of Bleeker Street. My mind reflects on the Greenwich Village of the 1960s when the intersection of Bleeker and MacDougal was the epicenter of folk artists and the counter culture. But college professors at the time point out that Greenwich Village was also filled with expensive residences and high-priced apartments. Today, expensive apartments abound. Even the Bowery sweeps up the indigenous street people, inviting in mostly investment bankers, lawyers but for the occasional artist.

I make my way towards Grand Central Station where I pick up the *New York Times* and hop on a train for the suburbs. Perusing through the paper to pass the time, I come upon a picture of an elderly man, dressed in traditional middle eastern garments, a full-length gray tunic and white turban, standing near gravesites. The article tells a tragic story. His whole family, wife, children, grandchildren, killed in a "friendly fire" incident in today's war. There are no words.

I wonder where Ralph is now. Although my high school crew, the fellas, gets together occasionally for a week of sun, surf and golf on the Outer Banks in North Carolina, Ralph is rarely mentioned. It's been decades since I last saw his father and his then, new wife. I hope Mister Albanese found, or made for himself, a separate peace.

I rest the paper on my lap and look out the window to pass the time until they announce our arrival at Katonah, my destination.

Elizabeth, my wife, meets me up at the train station as I step from the train's platform. She is still attractive and the means of all my joy. The sparkle in her blue eyes complement her smile as she walks towards me. An intelligent woman who is no stranger to hardship. She gravitates to joy by choice and disposition. She plants a kiss on my cheek. Her pleasant demeanor is infectious. It is a sunny afternoon made cool by a suburban breeze.

"The car is parked down by the church. Up for the walk?" She asks.

"Sure," I respond, "let's take the route past the library".

Walking in Katonah, one can almost see Jimmy Stewart and Donna Reed sitting on an old stone bench with a wooden seat. The bench rests on the grass island that separates the single-lane roads, one going north and the other south. Old evergreens and deciduous trees on the median provide a backdrop of color with seasonal yellows, reds and oranges.

The trees are the oldest living things in Katonah. Like sentinels, they greet you as you approach the town. They advise you that Katonah is not like the place from whence you came, nor that of your destination. Where you are, they whisper, is an old-time, American town at home with its past and present. The good town folk restore a civil war canon onto the median to remind one that freedom, like second chances, comes at a price.

It is a "hot town," according to the *New York Times'* real estate section. It is also an old town too. Uprooted from its origins and transplanted to a new place to make way for the New York City reservoir system. Things change. Katonah's past looks down from a picture in a small room on the second floor of the town library.

We reach the car.

"Hop in," Elizabeth says. "When we get home, you can help with dinner and put the girls to bed."

. . .

I hesitate at the threshold. To knock could be to awaken, to steal moments from her sleep. I hear the light cadence of her breath. It emboldens me. I push the door ajar. Subdued light offers little clarity. Her voice comes softly to my ears.

"Its OK dad. I'm awake."

With a soft shuffle of my soles, I cross the threshold into her room. The walls made soft by her choice of blue, offset the hard, wooden edges of the desk and chest of drawers. I lower myself slowly onto the edge of her bed, careful not to impinge upon her small slim frame.

"How was school today?" It's the end of the school year. I expect joy and good news given the advent of summer.

"Ok," she replies.

"Just OK?"

"The Italian teacher went up and down the rows of kids today, telling each smart kid that they should take Italian next year. The teacher passed over me."

"Who wants to take Italian anyway?" I add.

"It's my reading, especially in Italian. Why can't I read like everyone else? Why do I have to be different?"

"Well, I think," my thought racing for the words to put a gentle soul at ease, "it's because God wants you to be perfect."

There is a precious pause. I catch the light of the moon in her eyes as she begins to tear up.

"Tell me again about my gifts, Dad," she asks in a quiet whisper with a hint of a wounded heart.

"Well, you have lots of friends, good friends. A lot of people like you because of who you are and how you treat them. And you're good at soccer. You are on the varsity. You have that signature turn-around move that makes the crowd go crazy. And I think that you are very pretty. A lot of girls think that pretty is important. And you are smart. The teachers say that you will read fast someday. It's just gonna take you a little bit longer, that's all."

Her features loosen a bit, the brow unfurls.

I continue, "Barbara Chase is a good at soccer player, and she reads fast, but she's not really nice to people. Maybe it's because she doesn't know what it's like to be passed over."

I pause to check her expression before continuing. She appears pensive.

"This way you appreciate everyone else who is not a perfect student, or who is not good at sports, or feels 'less than' for some other reason. And that's important. Perhaps God made you this way because he wants you to be perfect, or closer to perfect."

"You are like your mother. You have a lot of friends and you get along with all types of people. I was not so gifted as you. School came easy to me but I was shy growing up. I envied people like you, comfortable with everyone, with lots of friends. That does not come natural to everyone."

"You have great gifts. You have the important gifts that make for a full and happy life. You will be alright."

A smile returns to her face. The subdued light in the room loses its chill and wraps around us like a warm blanket.

"Thanks, Dad."

I stand upright and tuck her in, like when she was a little kid. She laughs. I chuckle. I glance out the window. The moonlight blots out all the stars except one—the one that guides sailors and lost souls.

"Good night, sleep tight," I say as I navigate back out to the hall. I stop my steps to listen for the breathing of her two sisters, the sound of which fills the spaces within me.

I pass into my bedroom and see the soft shape of my wife beneath the covers. The moonlight reveals her slight figure and my ears record the rhythmic breath of a body at rest. I smile a satisfied smile with only a hint of disappointment. But tomorrow is another day and another night.

As a fall asleep I hear the faint creak of the stairs as angels scurry down and out the front door to report to another assignment in a galaxy far, far away, and a long, long time ago.

Goodnight Moon.

AFTERWORD
Eulogy for Eileen O'Toole

We have a lunch date in the city with friends and family. I enter the kitchen from the dining room indifferent to the black and white décor. My mother is standing in the center of the floor between the sink, the stove and the nook, a small section of the kitchen which consists of a table and pew-like benches. She is dressed for the event in a soft olive dress, a fashionable and trendy outfit for her elderly figure. The shoes too are trendy, pointed boots covered with an olive suede that abruptly end above the ankle.

She strikes a pose, hand on hip and the other placed coquettishly behind her coiffed hair—comic and endearing.

"Too fashionable?" she asks. "It's what all the girls are wearing," she purrs with an impish grin.

"You look fabulous, darling!" I smile back at her. All the world is a stage and I can't hide my amusement at one of the great comic actors of our time.

She begins a little tap dance accompanied by the clap of small wings as she fetters from sink to table, table to stove, stove to sink. Toe to heal, heal to toe, her feet clap the rhythm of the happy dance. Jesus joins in the little pas de deux. They are graceful together. He spins her, she twirls. They tap across the kitchen floor, down the steps, out the side entrance into the driveway, one long concrete slab with a strip of grass in the center. She taps on the cemented strip of ground and pirouettes over the grass onto the other strip of pavement, and then jumps back across, again and again. Tapping like Ginger Rogers and Fred Astaire, they dance past the white Ford station wagon, up and down the front stoop, over the sidewalk onto the street.

Mr. and Mrs. Thomas and their ten children come dancing out of their corner house onto the sidewalk and into the street. The company taps and twirls up towards the avenue. The O'Haras, a clan of twelve, empty from their house, dancing—their blonde hair reflecting the glow of a joyous sun. Tap, tap, slide goes the entourage, tap, tap slide up the street to the corner candy store.

Jesus nods to signal the start of the slow dance. She'll have none of it! She's gotta dance, dance, dance! Sinatra woulda wanted it this way. Liza Minnelli and Joel Grey applaud from the second-floor window of the red brick house across from the O'Haras. Now she looks and dances like a young Judy Garland. Jesus becomes Andrew Hardy as they tap, tap, slide and pirouette.

Jesus and Eileen O'Toole lead the troupe, twirling, tapping, two-stepping towards the avenue where her chariot of fire awaits. The whirling duo part from the entourage and tap in sixteenth time across the avenue to the bus stop in front of Mr. Jay's Appliance store. Jesus helps her board. She turns back and flashes a wide grin to the crowd, tossing her hat in the air.

She grabs the reins and flies into the sun and whispers her last words to me, "Dance. Dance. Dance!"

CPSIA information can be obtained
at www.ICGtesting.com
Printed in the USA
BVHW030209310122
627607BV00009B/127